Being in 2020

Releasing
what it was like to BE in 2020
Resetting
into 2021 and beyond
Through Lists, Be-oodles, Quotes, Conversations, and More!

ISBN 978-1-7360534-0-9

Using such sites as QuoteInvestigator® at quoteinvestigator.com, Wikiquote at https://en.wikiquote.org/wiki/Main_Page; BrainyQuote at https://www.brainyquote.com, as well as reference articles and books of quotations, care has been taken to ensure the accuracy of the quotes and poems used in this book. However, confirming the original source of a quote is not always simple or easy. In many instances, different resources have different conclusions. If you find any error, please feel free to email Kerry at **TheBeingJournals@gmail.com**.

Kerry Raleigh also hosts a podcast, Silver Lining Moments with Kerry. This podcast is found at http://silverliningmoments.libsyn.com and other podcast platforms. In addition to *The Being [Your Age/Me/in2020] Journal Series*, she created a guided journal: *Silver Lining Moments: A Practice of Gratitude & Resilience.*

At the time of publication of this journal, Kerry's website www.SilverLiningMoments.Com is under development. It is anticipated to be completed by December 2020. In the meantime, look for The Being Journals and Silver Lining Moments on social media or email Kerry.

Icons designed by various artsist on Freepik and Vecteezy.com
Cover design and page formatting by Sophie Coltburn for Kerry Raleigh.

ACKNOWLEDGEMENTS & APPRECIATION

When my niece, Jordan, turned 13, I didn't have money to get her a gift. So, instead of a gift, I made her a journal that celebrated and explored being 13 in a series of prompts and lists. A few months later, Christmas came and I still didn't have money to buy Christmas gifts for Jordan or her two sisters, Allie and Cori. I really liked the first Being 13 Journal. For their Christmas present, I promised them that I would: (1) create, publish, and sell the Being 13 Journal plus one Being Journal for every age from 5 to 18, (2) share the creative and entrepreneurial process with them, and (3) share the profits with them. From a time of limited money but a lot of love, these Being Journals were born.

Since then, Allie, Cori, and Jordan have reviewed my lists, selected quotes, and cover and page designs. They offered suggestions for the list prompts and helped choose which lists and which quotes to use with each Being Journal. Their mother and my sister, Kelly, also helped review the lists and quotes. My sister Kathy and my Mom reviewed the first draft and gave helpful comments and support. For this *Being in 2020* Journal, I also sought input from my good friend and therapist, Alice Amos (http://aliceamos.me). Without their help, my creative process would have been stalled to a halt as I endlessly toiled over the specific wording of each list, topics for the lists, or quotes to be used.

After having one of our good conversations, my friend Debbie suggested adding a conversation component to the Being in 2020 Journal experience. Knowing first hand the power of a good conversation, I liked this idea and added a Conversations & Connection section!

With her graphic design services, Sophie Coltburn created the look and feel for The Being Journals that captured my ideas and vision. Her creativity and graphic design skills are surpassed only by her patience as I re-worked and revised this Journal. These Being Journals would not have come into their being without her.

Allie, Cori, Jordan, Kelly, Kathy, Mom, Alice, Debbie and Sophie: This *Being in 2020* Journal would not have been completed without you. My heart is full of gratitude for each of you. Thank you!

As the Being Journals were born out of love for my nieces, they also come with love for humanity and for each of you Journalers. It is my hope that you find these lists, Be-oodles™, MyWi pages, and selected quotes fun, engaging, and reflective.

In fully BEING ourselves, our connection to ourselves and to others deepens. And, in this BEING, humanity thrives and love expands.

To your BEING,
Kerry

THIS IS YOUR JOURNAL

There is no right or wrong way; there is only your way for your journal.

- Complete the lists by yourself or with some friends
- Complete these lists quickly or slowly
- Keep your lists to yourself or share with others
- Add some Be-oodles™, color, drawings, stickers
- Complete the lists, write some notes, create some designs, color the pages – or not.
- Make it your own by completing it and using it however you want

THE LISTS: 21 LISTS FOR 2020…HUH?

Typically, the number of lists in the Being Journals corresponds to the age or number in the title. *Being 13* Journal has 13 lists of 13, the *Being 14* Journal has 14 lists of 14, so on and so forth. The *Being in 2020* Journal was originally going to have 20 lists of 10 because, well, 2,020 lists of 2,020 was too many and 20 lists still corresponded to the year 2020 and the title *Being in 2020*, and 10 spaces for each list just seemed to fit.

Then, I remembered something that Mr. Dombrowski, my neighbor/slash "running coach", taught me. When I was 12 or 13, I started to tag along with Mr. Dombrowski on his daily runs up and down our street. Instead of feeling pestered that I may slow him down or talk too much, he encouraged me. One lesson that extended beyond running was: end strong. No matter how our run went, Mr. Dombrowski always had me do a full sprint for the last 50-100 yards. He said that "if you end strong, you know that you have it in you to start strong on your next run."

So, the 21st list (and the 11 instead of 10, spaces for each list) in this *Being in 2020* Journal represents your full sprint towards the end of 2020. By ending this year strong through your list reflections, you know that you have it in you to start 2021 and beyond strong.

THIS IS YOUR JOURNAL ABOUT JUST BEING YOU.

No matter the number of lists or how the lists are completed or how the pages are filled, this journal is a celebration, exploration, and reflection of being you. You have nothing more to do than *Just Be* you.

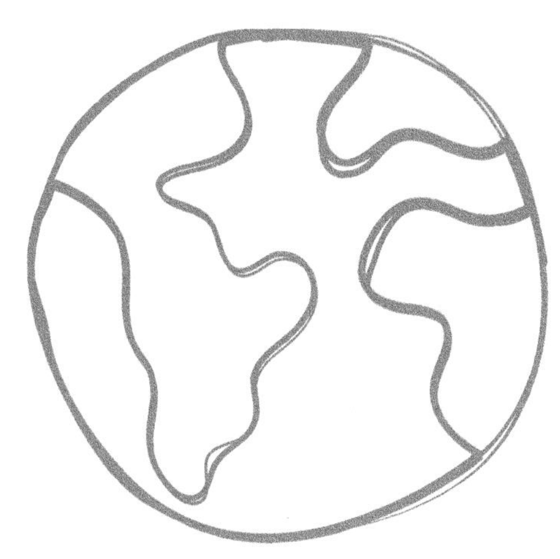

He is a wise man who does not grieve for the things which he has not, but rejoices for those which he has.

– Epictetus

BE-oodle™

BE-oodle™ – v. to still the mind through absent-minded doodling and allowing one to simply and fully Just Be.

BE-oodle™ – n. the mindfulness, stillness, calming feeling, and/or beauty created within one's self from simply and fully Just Being achieved through BE-oodling.

Other forms: BE-oodling

BE-oodle-ful™ – adj. (i) describing what is created by BE-oodling; (i) of having, or being filled with, the mindfulness, stillness, calming feeling, and/or beauty created within one's self from simply and fully Just Being from BE-oodling.

BE-oodling

BE-oodling

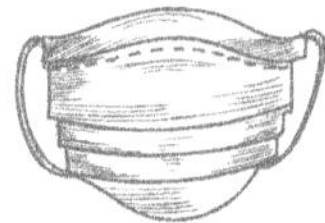

BE-oodle-ful

Gratitude

11 things that I am grateful for right now:

1 ___________________________________

2 ___________________________________

3 ___________________________________

4 ___________________________________

5 ___________________________________

6 ___________________________________

7 ___________________________________

8 ___________________________________

9 ___________________________________

10 ___________________________________

11 ___________________________________

MyWi
My Words, My Wisdom

Go ahead, let your wisdom out, your brilliance shine, your soul howl.
Write your own fortune cookie fortune, life mantra, quote, poem, song,
witty one-liner, sarcastic joke…you get the idea. This space - your words, your wisdom:

Quotes and poems of others are nice,
Ideas and inspiration abound.
Relying solely on them can be a vice,
For, within myself, the greatest wisdom is found.
- Kerry Raleigh

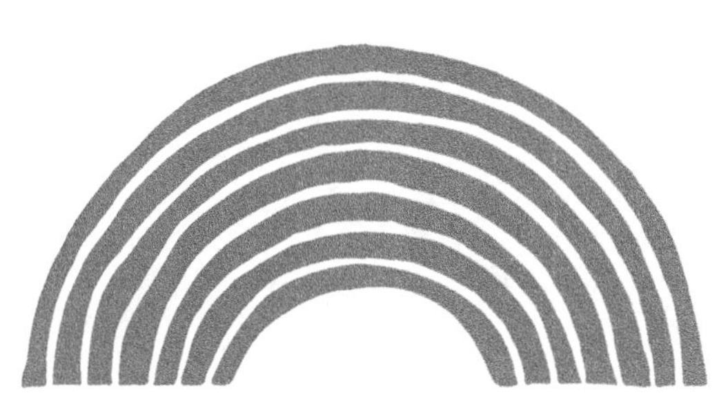

I'll be a candle holder, and look on.
The game was ne'er so fair,
and I am done.

– William Shakespeare

BE-oodle™

BE-oodle™ – v. to still the mind through absent-minded doodling and allowing one to simply and fully Just Be.

BE-oodle™ – n. the mindfulness, stillness, calming feeling, and/or beauty created within one's self from simply and fully Just Being achieved through BE-oodling.

Other forms: BE-oodling

BE-oodle-ful™ – adj. (i) describing what is created by BE-oodling; (i) of having, or being filled with, the mindfulness, stillness, calming feeling, and/or beauty created within one's self from simply and fully Just Being from BE-oodling.

BE-oodling

BE-oodling

BE-oodle-ful

Release

My 2020 venting list: all the things that, for lack of a better word,
just sucked in 2020:

1 _______________________________

2 _______________________________

3 _______________________________

4 _______________________________

5 _______________________________

6 _______________________________

7 _______________________________

8 _______________________________

9 _______________________________

10 _______________________________

11 _______________________________

MyWi
My Words, My Wisdom

Go ahead, let your wisdom out, your brilliance shine, your soul howl.
Write your own fortune cookie fortune, life mantra, quote, poem, song,
witty one-liner, sarcastic joke…you get the idea. This space - your words, your wisdom:

Quotes and poems of others are nice,
Ideas and inspiration abound.
Relying solely on them can be a vice,
For, within myself, the greatest wisdom is found.
- Kerry Raleigh

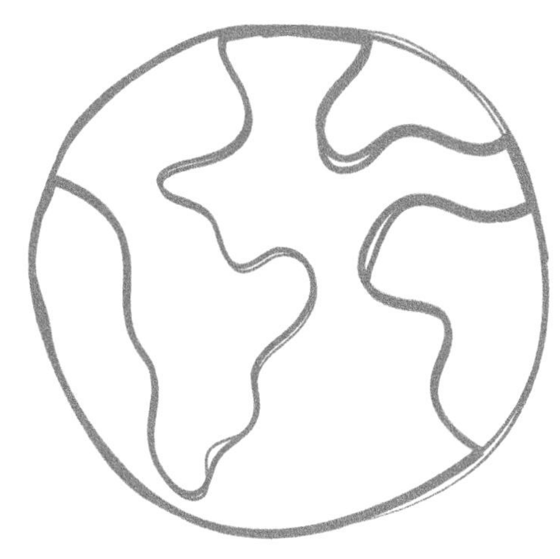

'Tis easy enough to be pleasant
When life flows along like a song;
But the man worth while is the one
who will smile
When everything goes dead wrong.

— Ella Wheeler Wilcox

BE-oodle™

BE-oodle™ – v. to still the mind through absent-minded doodling and allowing one to simply and fully Just Be.

BE-oodle™ – n. the mindfulness, stillness, calming feeling, and/or beauty created within one's self from simply and fully Just Being achieved through BE-oodling.

Other forms: BE-oodling

BE-oodle-ful™ – adj. (i) describing what is created by BE-oodling; (i) of having, or being filled with, the mindfulness, stillness, calming feeling, and/or beauty created within one's self from simply and fully Just Being from BE-oodling.

BE-oodling

BE-oodling

BE-oodle-ful

Hope

People, moments, or events that restored my belief in humanity in 2020:

1 ____

2 ____

3 ____

4 ____

5 ____

6 ____

7 ____

8 ____

9 ____

10 ____

11 ____

"Hope" is the thing with feathers
By Emily Dickinson

"Hope" is the thing with feathers -
That perches in the soul -
And sings the tune without the words -
And never stops - at all -

And sweetest - in the Gale - is heard -
And sore must be the storm -
That could abash the little Bird
That kept so many warm -

I've heard it in the chillest land -
And on the strangest Sea -
Yet - never - in Extremity,
It asked a crumb - of me.

MyWi
My Words, My Wisdom

Go ahead, let your wisdom out, your brilliance shine, your soul howl.
Write your own fortune cookie fortune, life mantra, quote, poem, song,
witty one-liner, sarcastic joke…you get the idea. This space - your words, your wisdom:

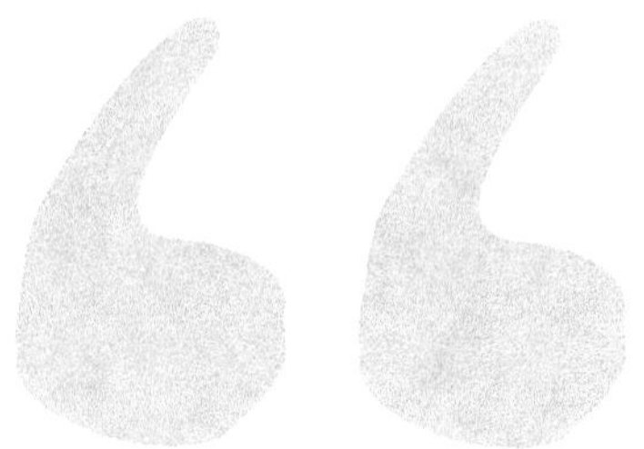

Quotes and poems of others are nice,
Ideas and inspiration abound.
Relying solely on them can be a vice,
For, within myself, the greatest wisdom is found.
- Kerry Raleigh

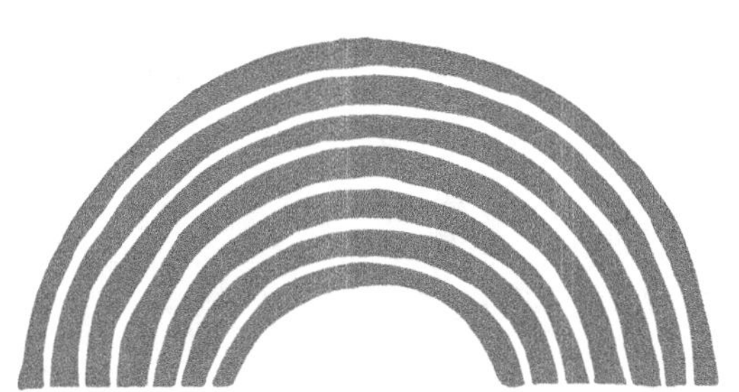

What soap is to the body,
laughter is to the soul.

— A Yiddish Proverb

BE-oodle™

BE-oodle™ – v. to still the mind through absent-minded doodling and allowing one to simply and fully Just Be.

BE-oodle™ – n. the mindfulness, stillness, calming feeling, and/or beauty created within one's self from simply and fully Just Being achieved through BE-oodling.

Other forms: BE-oodling

BE-oodle-ful™ – adj. (i) describing what is created by BE-oodling; (i) of having, or being filled with, the mindfulness, stillness, calming feeling, and/or beauty created within one's self from simply and fully Just Being from BE-oodling.

BE-oodling

BE-oodling

BE-oodle-ful

In a nutshell, it's all nuts!

Nicknames, jingles, slogans, memes, GIFs, or theme songs for 2020:

1 ____

2 ____

3 ____

4 ____

5 ____

6 ____

7 ____

8 ____

9 ____

10 ____

11 ____

MyWi
My Words, My Wisdom

Go ahead, let your wisdom out, your brilliance shine, your soul howl.
Write your own fortune cookie fortune, life mantra, quote, poem, song,
witty one-liner, sarcastic joke…you get the idea. This space - your words, your wisdom:

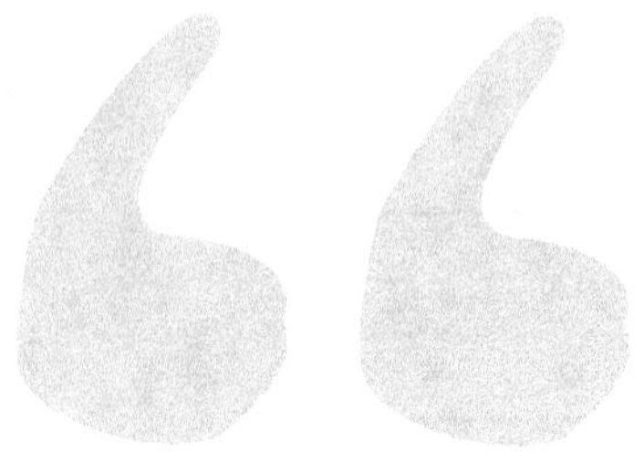

Quotes and poems of others are nice,
Ideas and inspiration abound.
Relying solely on them can be a vice,
For, within myself, the greatest wisdom is found.
- Kerry Raleigh

Wisdom begins in wonder.

– Socrates

BE-oodle™

BE-oodle™ – v. to still the mind through absent-minded doodling and allowing one to simply and fully Just Be.

BE-oodle™ – n. the mindfulness, stillness, calming feeling, and/or beauty created within one's self from simply and fully Just Being achieved through BE-oodling.

Other forms: BE-oodling

BE-oodle-ful™ – adj. (i) describing what is created by BE-oodling; (i) of having, or being filled with, the mindfulness, stillness, calming feeling, and/or beauty created within one's self from simply and fully Just Being from BE-oodling.

BE-oodling

BE-oodling

BE-oodle-ful

Science Matters

The statistics, charts, or science words that became part of my every day vocabulary in 2020:

1 _______________________________

2 _______________________________

3 _______________________________

4 _______________________________

5 _______________________________

6 _______________________________

7 _______________________________

8 _______________________________

9 _______________________________

10 _______________________________

11 _______________________________

MyWi
My Words, My Wisdom

Go ahead, let your wisdom out, your brilliance shine, your soul howl.
Write your own fortune cookie fortune, life mantra, quote, poem, song,
witty one-liner, sarcastic joke…you get the idea. This space - your words, your wisdom:

Quotes and poems of others are nice,
Ideas and inspiration abound.
Relying solely on them can be a vice,
For, within myself, the greatest wisdom is found.
- Kerry Raleigh

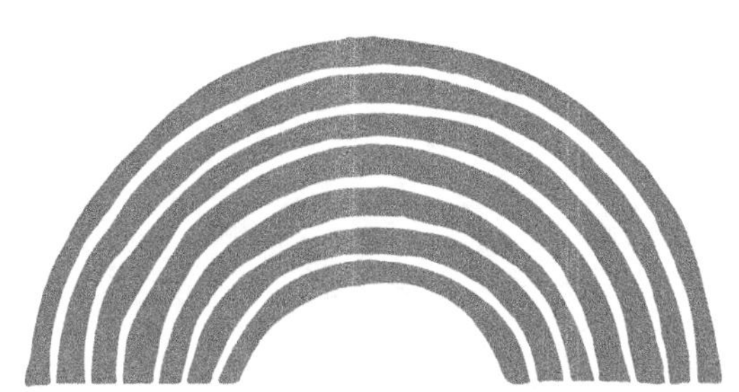

People are never so near
playing the fool as when they
think themselves wise.

— Lady Mary Wortley Montagu

BE-oodle™

BE-oodle™ – v. to still the mind through absent-minded doodling and allowing one to simply and fully Just Be.

BE-oodle™ – n. the mindfulness, stillness, calming feeling, and/or beauty created within one's self from simply and fully Just Being achieved through BE-oodling.

Other forms: BE-oodling

BE-oodle-ful™ – adj. (i) describing what is created by BE-oodling; (i) of having, or being filled with, the mindfulness, stillness, calming feeling, and/or beauty created within one's self from simply and fully Just Being from BE-oodling.

BE-oodling

BE-oodling

BE-oodle-ful

Distorted Distractions

Conspiracy theories about 2020:

1.

2.

3.

4.

5.

6.

7.

8.

9.

10.

11.

MyWi
My Words, My Wisdom

Go ahead, let your wisdom out, your brilliance shine, your soul howl.
Write your own fortune cookie fortune, life mantra, quote, poem, song,
witty one-liner, sarcastic joke…you get the idea. This space - your words, your wisdom:

Quotes and poems of others are nice,
Ideas and inspiration abound.
Relying solely on them can be a vice,
For, within myself, the greatest wisdom is found.
- Kerry Raleigh

When there are thoughts, it is distraction: when there are no thoughts, it is meditation.

— Ramana Maharshi

BE-oodle™

BE-oodle™ – v. to still the mind through absent-minded doodling and allowing one to simply and fully Just Be.

BE-oodle™ – n. the mindfulness, stillness, calming feeling, and/or beauty created within one's self from simply and fully Just Being achieved through BE-oodling.

Other forms: BE-oodling

BE-oodle-ful™ – adj. (i) describing what is created by BE-oodling; (i) of having, or being filled with, the mindfulness, stillness, calming feeling, and/or beauty created within one's self from simply and fully Just Being from BE-oodling.

BE-oodling

BE-oodling

BE-oodle-ful

Welcomed Distractions

The TV shows, podcasts, movies, or songs that I streamed in 2020:

1

2

3

4

5

6

7

8

9

10

11

MyWi
My Words, My Wisdom

Go ahead, let your wisdom out, your brilliance shine, your soul howl.
Write your own fortune cookie fortune, life mantra, quote, poem, song,
witty one-liner, sarcastic joke…you get the idea. This space - your words, your wisdom:

Quotes and poems of others are nice,
Ideas and inspiration abound.
Relying solely on them can be a vice,
For, within myself, the greatest wisdom is found.
- Kerry Raleigh

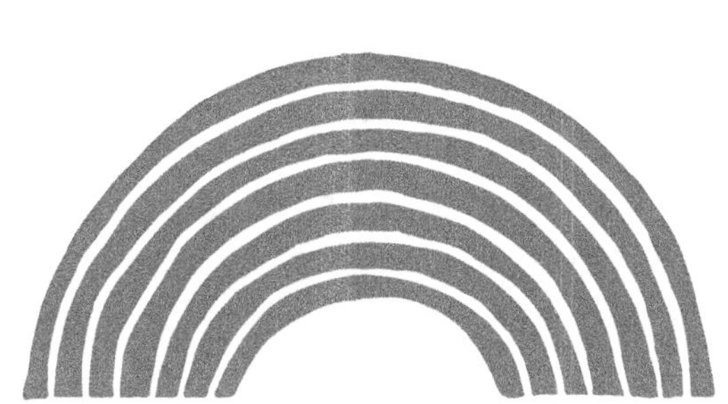

This world is but canvas to our imaginations.

— Henry David Thoreau

BE-oodle™

BE-oodle™ – v. to still the mind through absent-minded doodling and allowing one to simply and fully Just Be.

BE-oodle™ – n. the mindfulness, stillness, calming feeling, and/or beauty created within one's self from simply and fully Just Being achieved through BE-oodling.

Other forms: BE-oodling

BE-oodle-ful™ – adj. (i) describing what is created by BE-oodling; (i) of having, or being filled with, the mindfulness, stillness, calming feeling, and/or beauty created within one's self from simply and fully Just Being from BE-oodling.

BE-oodling

BE-oodling

BE-oodle-ful

Shut the front door! No, seriously, shut the front door.

Signs from 2020 that we may very well just be in a sci-fi, dystopian-esque movie:

1 ____

2 ____

3 ____

4 ____

5 ____

6 ____

7 ____

8 ____

9 ____

10 ____

11 ____

MyWi
My Words, My Wisdom

Go ahead, let your wisdom out, your brilliance shine, your soul howl.
Write your own fortune cookie fortune, life mantra, quote, poem, song,
witty one-liner, sarcastic joke…you get the idea. This space - your words, your wisdom:

Quotes and poems of others are nice,
Ideas and inspiration abound.
Relying solely on them can be a vice,
For, within myself, the greatest wisdom is found.
- Kerry Raleigh

Life imitates art far more than
art imitates Life.

— Oscar Wilde

BE-oodle™

BE-oodle™ – v. to still the mind through absent-minded doodling and allowing one to simply and fully Just Be.

BE-oodle™ – n. the mindfulness, stillness, calming feeling, and/or beauty created within one's self from simply and fully Just Being achieved through BE-oodling.

Other forms: BE-oodling

BE-oodle-ful™ – adj. (i) describing what is created by BE-oodling; (i) of having, or being filled with, the mindfulness, stillness, calming feeling, and/or beauty created within one's self from simply and fully Just Being from BE-oodling.

BE-oodling

BE-oodling

BE-oodle-ful

And, the Oscar goes to...

If my life in 2020 was a movie, the key scenes would be:

1 ____

2 ____

3 ____

4 ____

5 ____

6 ____

7 ____

8 ____

9 ____

10 ____

11 ____

MyWi
My Words, My Wisdom

Go ahead, let your wisdom out, your brilliance shine, your soul howl.
Write your own fortune cookie fortune, life mantra, quote, poem, song,
witty one-liner, sarcastic joke…you get the idea. This space - your words, your wisdom:

Quotes and poems of others are nice,
Ideas and inspiration abound.
Relying solely on them can be a vice,
For, within myself, the greatest wisdom is found.
- Kerry Raleigh

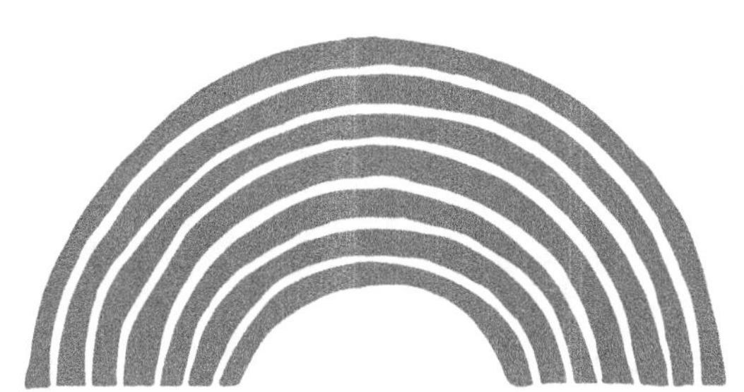

Everything has beauty,
but not everyone sees it.

— Confucius

BE-oodle™

BE-oodle™ – v. to still the mind through absent-minded doodling and allowing one to simply and fully Just Be.

BE-oodle™ – n. the mindfulness, stillness, calming feeling, and/or beauty created within one's self from simply and fully Just Being achieved through BE-oodling.

Other forms: BE-oodling

BE-oodle-ful™ – adj. (i) describing what is created by BE-oodling; (i) of having, or being filled with, the mindfulness, stillness, calming feeling, and/or beauty created within one's self from simply and fully Just Being from BE-oodling.

BE-oodling

BE-oodling

BE-oodle-ful

A Strange New World

From Zoom meetings to toilet paper rationing, ways life changed in 2020:

1

2

3

4

5

6

7

8

9

10

11

What is Poison?
Musings by Rumi

What is poison?
Anything which is more than our necessity is poison.
It may be power, wealth, hunger, ego, greed, laziness, love, ambition,
hate or anything.

What Is Fear?
Non-Acceptance of uncertainty.
If we accept that uncertainty, it becomes adventure.

What Is Envy?
Non-Acceptance pf good in others,
If we accept that good, it becomes inspiration.

What Is Anger?
Non-Acceptance of things which are beyond our control.
If we accept, it becomes tolerance.

What Is Hatred?
Non-Acceptance of person as he is.
If we accept person unconditionally, it becomes love.

MyWi
My Words, My Wisdom

Go ahead, let your wisdom out, your brilliance shine, your soul howl.
Write your own fortune cookie fortune, life mantra, quote, poem, song,
witty one-liner, sarcastic joke…you get the idea. This space - your words, your wisdom:

Quotes and poems of others are nice,
Ideas and inspiration abound.
Relying solely on them can be a vice,
For, within myself, the greatest wisdom is found.
- Kerry Raleigh

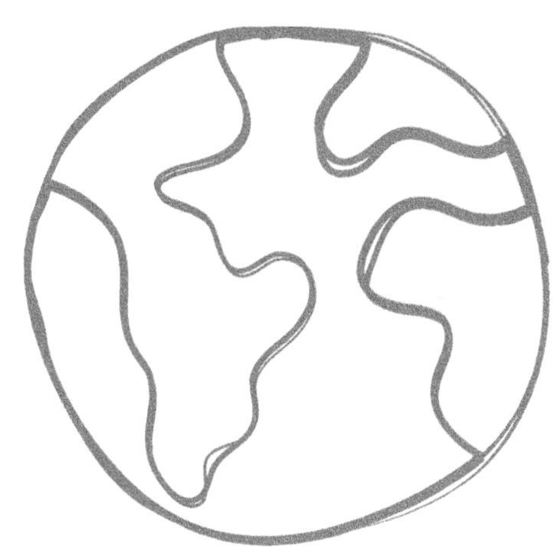

You see things; and you say, 'Why?'
But I dream things that never were;
and I say, 'Why not?'

– George Bernard Shaw
(The Serpent in Act I of Back to Methuselah)

BE-oodle™

BE-oodle™ – v. to still the mind through absent-minded doodling and allowing one to simply and fully Just Be.

BE-oodle™ – n. the mindfulness, stillness, calming feeling, and/or beauty created within one's self from simply and fully Just Being achieved through BE-oodling.

Other forms: BE-oodling

BE-oodle-ful™ – adj. (i) describing what is created by BE-oodling; (i) of having, or being filled with, the mindfulness, stillness, calming feeling, and/or beauty created within one's self from simply and fully Just Being from BE-oodling.

BE-oodling

BE-oodling

BE-oodle-ful

Resetting Normal

The new way of doing things: the parts of, or lessons from, 2020 that I will keep for myself and/or for the world:

1 ____

2 ____

3 ____

4 ____

5 ____

6 ____

7 ____

8 ____

9 ____

10 ____

11 ____

MyWi
My Words, My Wisdom

Go ahead, let your wisdom out, your brilliance shine, your soul howl.
Write your own fortune cookie fortune, life mantra, quote, poem, song,
witty one-liner, sarcastic joke…you get the idea. This space - your words, your wisdom:

Quotes and poems of others are nice,
Ideas and inspiration abound.
Relying solely on them can be a vice,
For, within myself, the greatest wisdom is found.
- Kerry Raleigh

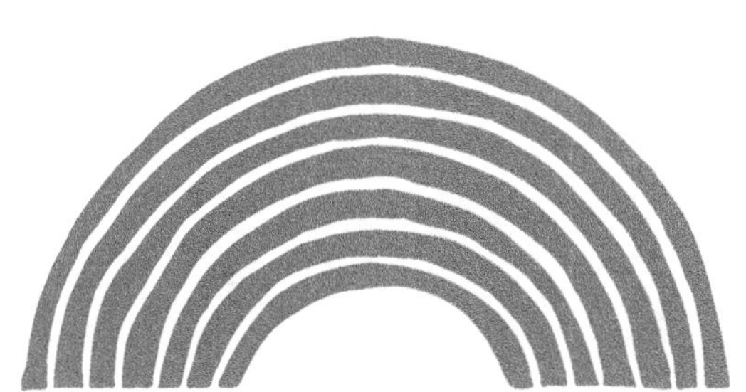

My life has been full of terrible
misfortunes most of which
never happened.

– Various People*

*Variations of this quote were attributed to different people from different times including: James A. Garfield,
Martin Farquhar Tupper, Seneca, Thomas Jefferson, Sir Daniel Wilson, Thomas Dixon Jr., Josh Billings,
Mark Twain, Michel de Montaigne.
See https://quoteinvestigator.com/2013/10/04/never-happened/#return-note-7370-14

BE-oodle™

BE-oodle™ – v. to still the mind through absent-minded doodling and allowing one to simply and fully Just Be.

BE-oodle™ – n. the mindfulness, stillness, calming feeling, and/or beauty created within one's self from simply and fully Just Being achieved through BE-oodling.

Other forms: BE-oodling

BE-oodle-ful™ – adj. (i) describing what is created by BE-oodling; (i) of having, or being filled with, the mindfulness, stillness, calming feeling, and/or beauty created within one's self from simply and fully Just Being from BE-oodling.

BE-oodling

BE-oodling

BE-oodle-ful

Sleepless Nights

Things that kept me up at night with worry, fear, or anxiety in 2020:

1 _______________________________________

2 _______________________________________

3 _______________________________________

4 _______________________________________

5 _______________________________________

6 _______________________________________

7 _______________________________________

8 _______________________________________

9 _______________________________________

10 _______________________________________

11 _______________________________________

MyWi
My Words, My Wisdom

Go ahead, let your wisdom out, your brilliance shine, your soul howl.
Write your own fortune cookie fortune, life mantra, quote, poem, song,
witty one-liner, sarcastic joke…you get the idea. This space - your words, your wisdom:

Quotes and poems of others are nice,
Ideas and inspiration abound.
Relying solely on them can be a vice,
For, within myself, the greatest wisdom is found.
- Kerry Raleigh

You have your way. I have my way. As for the right way, the correct way, and the only way, it does not exist.

– Friedrich Nietzsche[*]

*This quote may be paraphrased from: ""This–is now my way,–where is yours?" Thus did I answer those who asked me "the way." For the way–it doth not exist!" as discussed in Quote Investigator website at https://quoteinvestigator.com/2020/06/07/my-truth/#more-437914

BE-oodle™

BE-oodle™ – v. to still the mind through absent-minded doodling and allowing one to simply and fully Just Be.

BE-oodle™ – n. the mindfulness, stillness, calming feeling, and/or beauty created within one's self from simply and fully Just Being achieved through BE-oodling.

Other forms: BE-oodling

BE-oodle-ful™ – adj. (i) describing what is created by BE-oodling; (i) of having, or being filled with, the mindfulness, stillness, calming feeling, and/or beauty created within one's self from simply and fully Just Being from BE-oodling.

BE-oodling

BE-oodling

BE-oodle-ful

Triggers

People or events that triggered me in 2020:

1 ___________________________________

2 ___________________________________

3 ___________________________________

4 ___________________________________

5 ___________________________________

6 ___________________________________

7 ___________________________________

8 ___________________________________

9 ___________________________________

10 ___________________________________

11 ___________________________________

MyWi
My Words, My Wisdom

Go ahead, let your wisdom out, your brilliance shine, your soul howl.
Write your own fortune cookie fortune, life mantra, quote, poem, song,
witty one-liner, sarcastic joke…you get the idea. This space - your words, your wisdom:

Quotes and poems of others are nice,
Ideas and inspiration abound.
Relying solely on them can be a vice,
For, within myself, the greatest wisdom is found.
- Kerry Raleigh

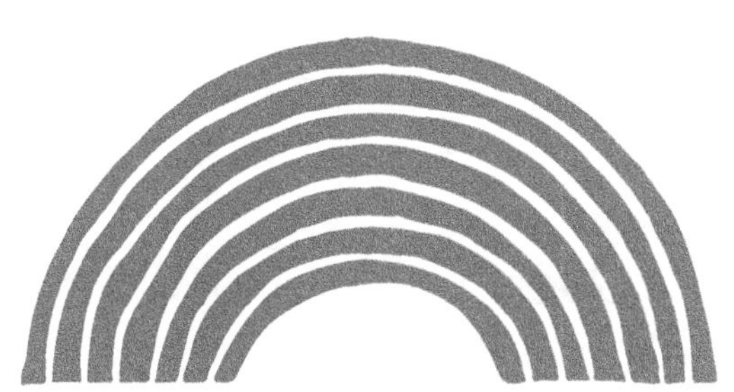

Courage is the price that life exacts for granting peace.

– Amelia Earhart

BE-oodle™

BE-oodle™ – v. to still the mind through absent-minded doodling and allowing one to simply and fully Just Be.

BE-oodle™ – n. the mindfulness, stillness, calming feeling, and/or beauty created within one's self from simply and fully Just Being achieved through BE-oodling.

Other forms: BE-oodling

BE-oodle-ful™ – adj. (i) describing what is created by BE-oodling; (i) of having, or being filled with, the mindfulness, stillness, calming feeling, and/or beauty created within one's self from simply and fully Just Being from BE-oodling.

BE-oodling

BE-oodling

BE-oodle-ful

Traumas

Times I felt like I was falling or that I might break in 2020:

1 ____________________________________

2 ____________________________________

3 ____________________________________

4 ____________________________________

5 ____________________________________

6 ____________________________________

7 ____________________________________

8 ____________________________________

9 ____________________________________

10 ____________________________________

11 ____________________________________

MyWi
My Words, My Wisdom

Go ahead, let your wisdom out, your brilliance shine, your soul howl.
Write your own fortune cookie fortune, life mantra, quote, poem, song,
witty one-liner, sarcastic joke…you get the idea. This space - your words, your wisdom:

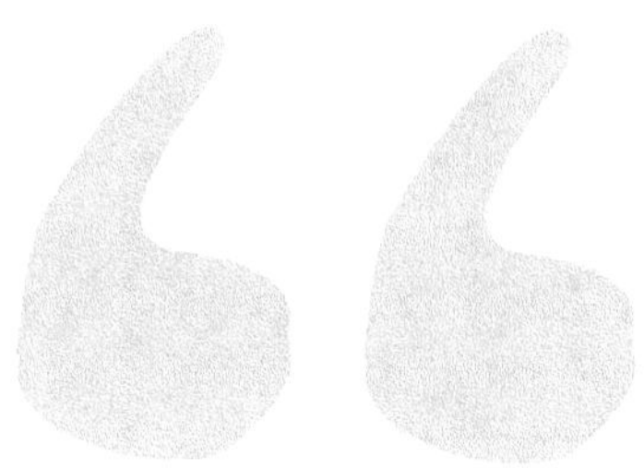

Quotes and poems of others are nice,
Ideas and inspiration abound.
Relying solely on them can be a vice,
For, within myself, the greatest wisdom is found.
- *Kerry Raleigh*

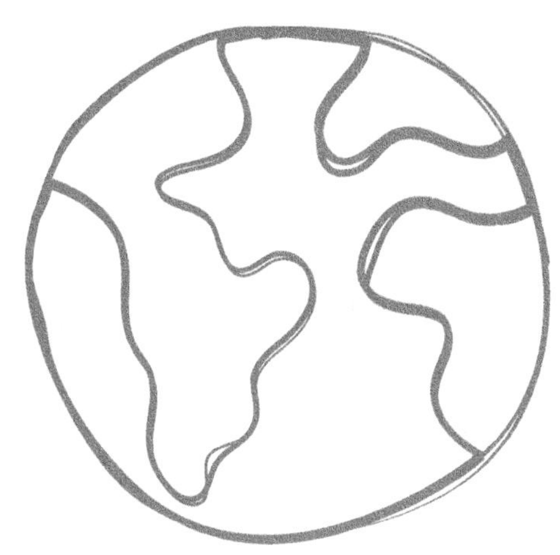

Sometimes all it takes is a tall tree.

— Kerry Raleigh

BE-oodle™

BE-oodle™ – v. to still the mind through absent-minded doodling and allowing one to simply and fully Just Be.

BE-oodle™ – n. the mindfulness, stillness, calming feeling, and/or beauty created within one's self from simply and fully Just Being achieved through BE-oodling.

Other forms: BE-oodling

BE-oodle-ful™ – adj. (i) describing what is created by BE-oodling; (i) of having, or being filled with, the mindfulness, stillness, calming feeling, and/or beauty created within one's self from simply and fully Just Being from BE-oodling.

BE-oodling

BE-oodling

BE-oodle-ful

Resilience Building

Practices or ways that I worked through my traumas, triggers, and sleepless nights or stayed standing when I felt like I was falling:

1 ____

2 ____

3 ____

4 ____

5 ____

6 ____

7 ____

8 ____

9 ____

10 ____

11 ____

MyWi
My Words, My Wisdom

Go ahead, let your wisdom out, your brilliance shine, your soul howl.
Write your own fortune cookie fortune, life mantra, quote, poem, song,
witty one-liner, sarcastic joke…you get the idea. This space - your words, your wisdom:

Quotes and poems of others are nice,
Ideas and inspiration abound.
Relying solely on them can be a vice,
For, within myself, the greatest wisdom is found.
- *Kerry Raleigh*

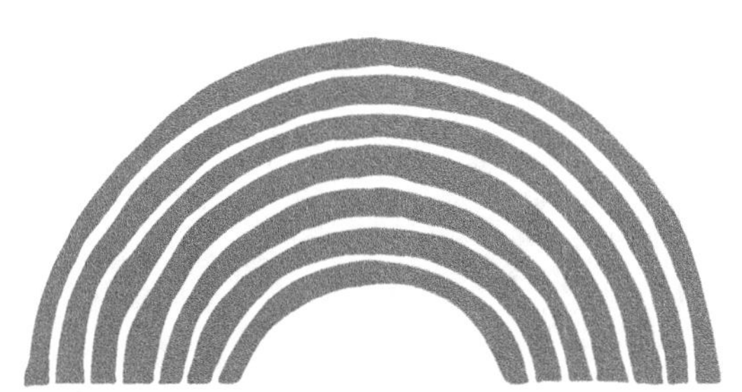

I wish I could show you when you are lonely or in darkness the astonishing light of your own being.

— Hafiz (aka Hafez)

BE-oodle™

BE-oodle™ – v. to still the mind through absent-minded doodling and allowing one to simply and fully Just Be.

BE-oodle™ – n. the mindfulness, stillness, calming feeling, and/or beauty created within one's self from simply and fully Just Being achieved through BE-oodling.

Other forms: BE-oodling

BE-oodle-ful™ – adj. (i) describing what is created by BE-oodling; (i) of having, or being filled with, the mindfulness, stillness, calming feeling, and/or beauty created within one's self from simply and fully Just Being from BE-oodling.

BE-oodling

BE-oodling

BE-oodle-ful

Saying Goodbye

Things, ideas, beliefs, relationships, or loved ones I let go or lost in 2020:

1 ____

2 ____

3 ____

4 ____

5 ____

6 ____

7 ____

8 ____

9 ____

10 ____

11 ____

MyWi
My Words, My Wisdom

Go ahead, let your wisdom out, your brilliance shine, your soul howl.
Write your own fortune cookie fortune, life mantra, quote, poem, song,
witty one-liner, sarcastic joke…you get the idea. This space - your words, your wisdom:

Quotes and poems of others are nice,
Ideas and inspiration abound.
Relying solely on them can be a vice,
For, within myself, the greatest wisdom is found.
- *Kerry Raleigh*

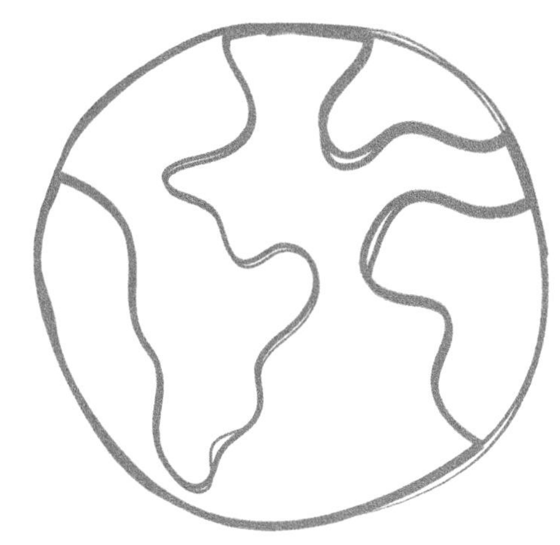

We are what we repeatedly do.
Excellence then is not an act, but a habit.

— Aristotle

BE-oodle™

BE-oodle™ – v. to still the mind through absent-minded doodling and allowing one to simply and fully Just Be.

BE-oodle™ – n. the mindfulness, stillness, calming feeling, and/or beauty created within one's self from simply and fully Just Being achieved through BE-oodling.

Other forms: BE-oodling

BE-oodle-ful™ – adj. (i) describing what is created by BE-oodling; (i) of having, or being filled with, the mindfulness, stillness, calming feeling, and/or beauty created within one's self from simply and fully Just Being from BE-oodling.

BE-oodling

BE-oodling

BE-oodle-ful

Living Anew

New things, skills, hobbies, ideas, beliefs, relationships, or loved ones
I picked up in 2020:

1. ____

2. ____

3. ____

4. ____

5. ____

6. ____

7. ____

8. ____

9. ____

10. ____

11. ____

MyWi
My Words. My Wisdom

Go ahead, let your wisdom out, your brilliance shine, your soul howl.
Write your own fortune cookie fortune, life mantra, quote, poem, song,
witty one-liner, sarcastic joke…you get the idea. This space - your words, your wisdom:

Quotes and poems of others are nice,
Ideas and inspiration abound.
Relying solely on them can be a vice,
For, within myself, the greatest wisdom is found.
- Kerry Raleigh

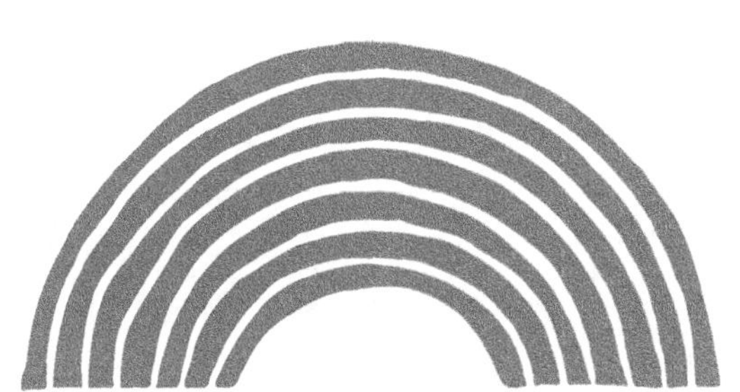

As long as you live,
keep learning how to live.

— Seneca

BE-oodle™

BE-oodle™ – v. to still the mind through absent-minded doodling and allowing one to simply and fully Just Be.

BE-oodle™ – n. the mindfulness, stillness, calming feeling, and/or beauty created within one's self from simply and fully Just Being achieved through BE-oodling.

Other forms: BE-oodling

BE-oodle-ful™ – adj. (i) describing what is created by BE-oodling; (i) of having, or being filled with, the mindfulness, stillness, calming feeling, and/or beauty created within one's self from simply and fully Just Being from BE-oodling.

BE-oodling

BE-oodling

BE-oodle-ful

Hello there, Sunshine!

Things I learned about myself in 2020:

1 _______________________________________

2 _______________________________________

3 _______________________________________

4 _______________________________________

5 _______________________________________

6 _______________________________________

7 _______________________________________

8 _______________________________________

9 _______________________________________

10 _______________________________________

11 _______________________________________

MyWi
My Words, My Wisdom

Go ahead, let your wisdom out, your brilliance shine, your soul howl.
Write your own fortune cookie fortune, life mantra, quote, poem, song,
witty one-liner, sarcastic joke…you get the idea. This space - your words, your wisdom:

Quotes and poems of others are nice,
Ideas and inspiration abound.
Relying solely on them can be a vice,
For, within myself, the greatest wisdom is found.
- Kerry Raleigh

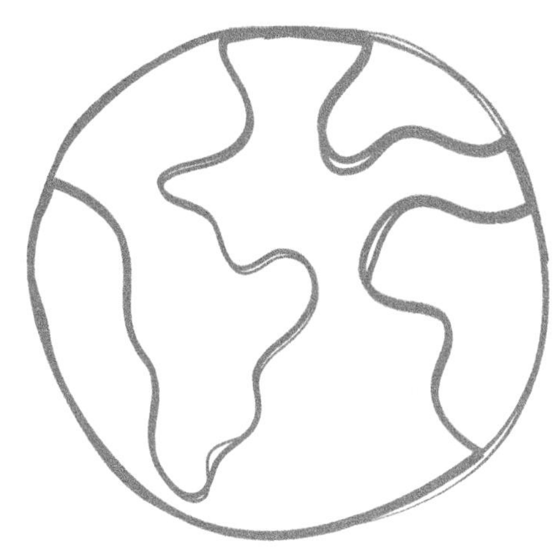

There are two ways of spreading light: to be the candle, or the mirror that reflects it.

– Edith Wharton

BE-oodle™

BE-oodle™ – v. to still the mind through absent-minded doodling and allowing one to simply and fully Just Be.

BE-oodle™ – n. the mindfulness, stillness, calming feeling, and/or beauty created within one's self from simply and fully Just Being achieved through BE-oodling.

Other forms: BE-oodling

BE-oodle-ful™ – adj. (i) describing what is created by BE-oodling; (i) of having, or being filled with, the mindfulness, stillness, calming feeling, and/or beauty created within one's self from simply and fully Just Being from BE-oodling.

BE-oodling

BE-oodling

BE-oodle-ful

Together

Ways the world connected in 2020:

1 _______________________________________

2 _______________________________________

3 _______________________________________

4 _______________________________________

5 _______________________________________

6 _______________________________________

7 _______________________________________

8 _______________________________________

9 _______________________________________

10 _______________________________________

11 _______________________________________

MyWi
My Words, My Wisdom

Go ahead, let your wisdom out, your brilliance shine, your soul howl.
Write your own fortune cookie fortune, life mantra, quote, poem, song,
witty one-liner, sarcastic joke…you get the idea. This space - your words, your wisdom:

Quotes and poems of others are nice,
Ideas and inspiration abound.
Relying solely on them can be a vice,
For, within myself, the greatest wisdom is found.
- Kerry Raleigh

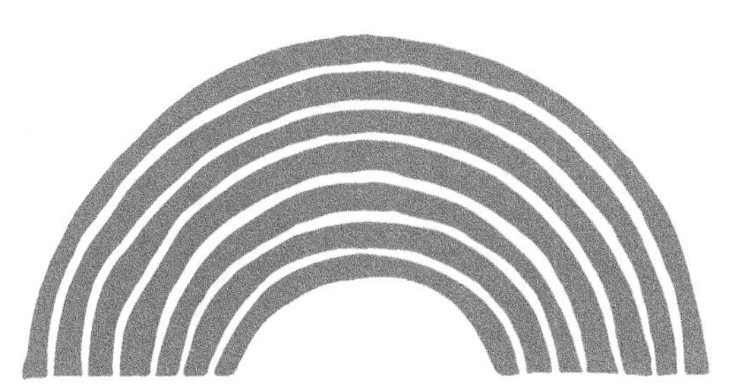

If we had no winter, the spring would not be so pleasant; if we did not sometimes taste of adversity, prosperity would not be so welcome.

– Anne Bradstreet

BE-oodle™

BE-oodle™ – v. to still the mind through absent-minded doodling and allowing one to simply and fully Just Be.

BE-oodle™ – n. the mindfulness, stillness, calming feeling, and/or beauty created within one's self from simply and fully Just Being achieved through BE-oodling.

Other forms: BE-oodling

BE-oodle-ful™ – adj. (i) describing what is created by BE-oodling; (i) of having, or being filled with, the mindfulness, stillness, calming feeling, and/or beauty created within one's self from simply and fully Just Being from BE-oodling.

BE-oodling

BE-oodling

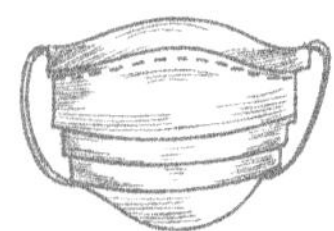

BE-oodle-ful

Getting It Right (or as is so often eloquently put, Nailed it!)

Words that complete this sentence, I am proud of my 2020 self for:

1 ____

2 ____

3 ____

4 ____

5 ____

6 ____

7 ____

8 ____

9 ____

10 ____

11 ____

MyWi
My Words, My Wisdom

Go ahead, let your wisdom out, your brilliance shine, your soul howl.
Write your own fortune cookie fortune, life mantra, quote, poem, song,
witty one-liner, sarcastic joke…you get the idea. This space - your words, your wisdom:

Quotes and poems of others are nice,
Ideas and inspiration abound.
Relying solely on them can be a vice,
For, within myself, the greatest wisdom is found.
- Kerry Raleigh

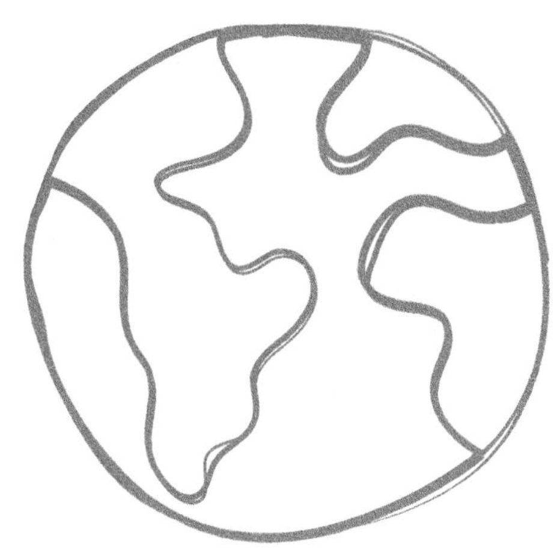

Beautiful.

— Elizabeth Barrett Browning
(when asked how she was feeling)

BE-oodle™

BE-oodle™ – v. to still the mind through absent-minded doodling and allowing one to simply and fully Just Be.

BE-oodle™ – n. the mindfulness, stillness, calming feeling, and/or beauty created within one's self from simply and fully Just Being achieved through BE-oodling.

Other forms: BE-oodling

BE-oodle-ful™ – adj. (i) describing what is created by BE-oodling; (i) of having, or being filled with, the mindfulness, stillness, calming feeling, and/or beauty created within one's self from simply and fully Just Being from BE-oodling.

BE-oodling

BE-oodling

BE-oodle-ful

"I"

Words that complete this sentence, I AM:

1 _______________________________

2 _______________________________

3 _______________________________

4 _______________________________

5 _______________________________

6 _______________________________

7 _______________________________

8 _______________________________

9 _______________________________

10 _______________________________

11 _______________________________

Just Be
By Kerry Raleigh

Be alive
Be brave, Be compassionate
Be daring, Be empowering, Be free
Be grateful, Be honest, Be inspired, Be joyous
Be kind, Be loving, Be magical, Be natural, Be original, Be prosperous,
Be quirky, Be receptive, Be silly, Be talented, Be useful, Be visionary,
Be wise, Be xenial, Be youthful, Be zany
Be, Be, Be - oh so many Be's to Be!

Be all these things and more they say
A different way to be for every moment of every day
Parents, teachers, bosses, social media, and friends
The list of the ways they say "to be" never ends
Some are natural and come with ease
Others don't fit but are merely being to please
But, in trying to check-off all the be's from every list
I completely miss the gist
The most important list is written within me
Oh, the infinite ways to be
From all this, here is the message I take
It's not about what they say or the lists I make
For all this trying puts me in a tizzy
Frazzled to the point of feeling dizzy
When this happens, for me and my best, I know
Breathe-in, breathe out, AHHH - let go
This is when I truly can
Just Be
And say
I
AM

I
Keep it going.
Be-oodle™
List
Create
Be
Be
Am
Just
These pages are all you for you. Fill them with your lists, your favorite quotes,
your designs, your scribbles or sketches. They are for you to *Just* Be You.

MyWi
My Words, My Wisdom

Go ahead, let your wisdom out, your brilliance shine, your soul howl.
Write your own fortune cookie fortune, life mantra, quote, poem, song,
witty one-liner, sarcastic joke…you get the idea. This space - your words, your wisdom:

Quotes and poems of others are nice,
Ideas and inspiration abound.
Relying solely on them can be a vice,
For, within myself, the greatest wisdom is found.
- *Kerry Raleigh*

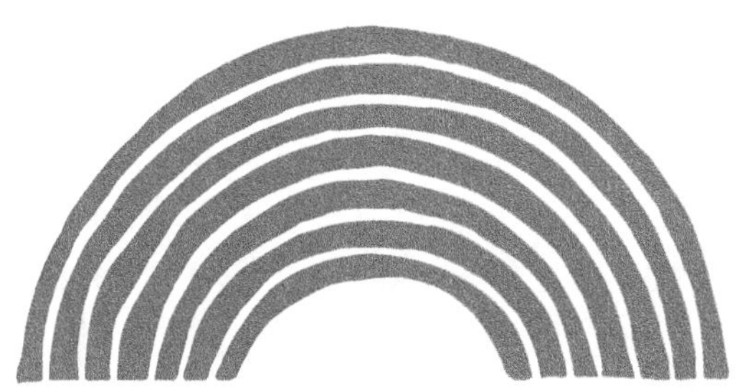

BE-oodle™

BE-oodle™ – v. to still the mind through absent-minded doodling and allowing one to simply and fully Just Be.

BE-oodle™ – n. the mindfulness, stillness, calming feeling, and/or beauty created within one's self from simply and fully Just Being achieved through BE-oodling.

Other forms: BE-oodling

BE-oodle-ful™ – adj. (i) describing what is created by BE-oodling; (i) of having, or being filled with, the mindfulness, stillness, calming feeling, and/or beauty created within one's self from simply and fully Just Being from BE-oodling.

BE-oodling

BE-oodling

BE-oodle-ful

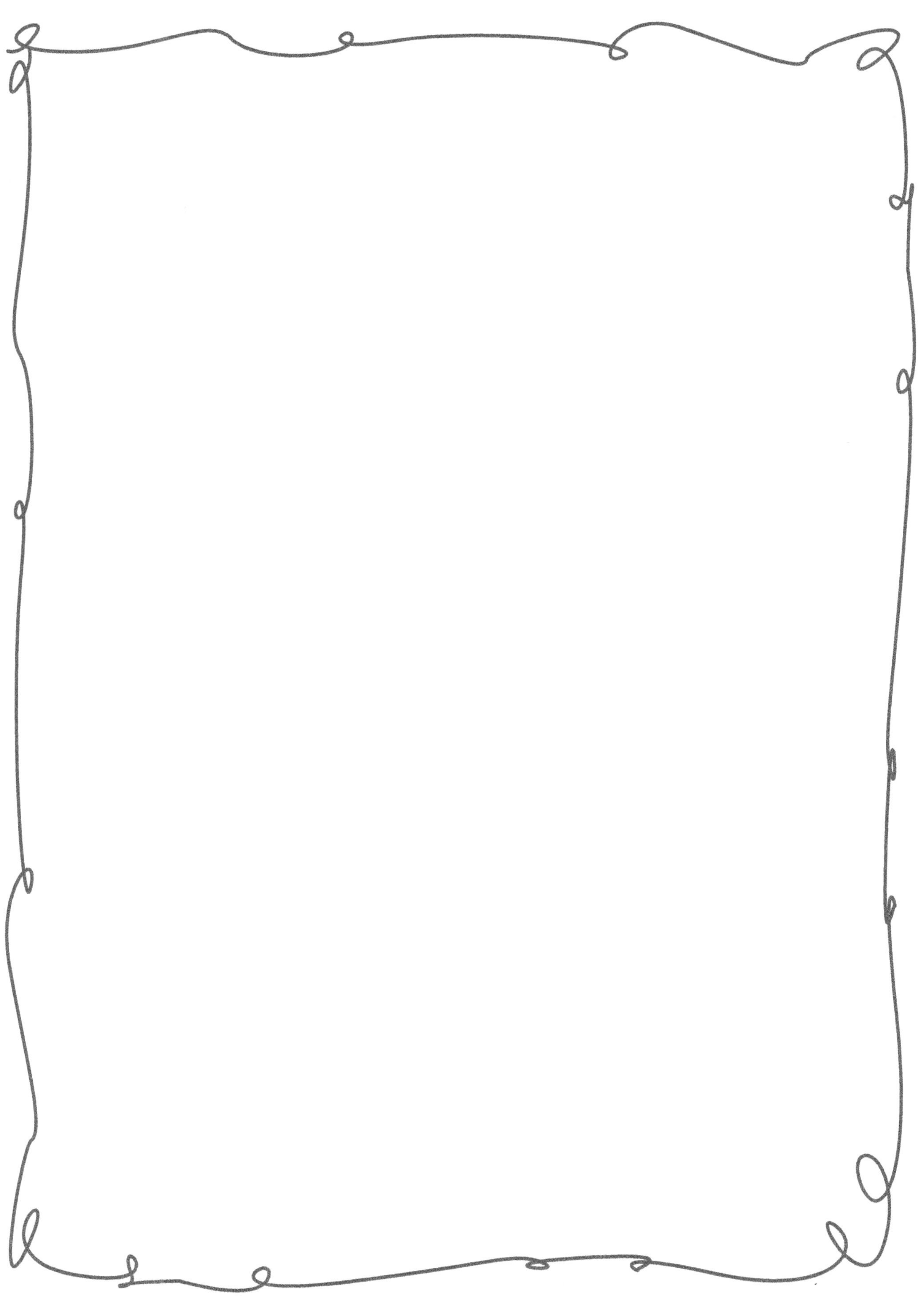

BE-oodle™

BE-oodle™ – v. to still the mind through absent-minded doodling and allowing one to simply and fully Just Be.

BE-oodle™ – n. the mindfulness, stillness, calming feeling, and/or beauty created within one's self from simply and fully Just Being achieved through BE-oodling.

Other forms: BE-oodling

BE-oodle-ful™ – adj. (i) describing what is created by BE-oodling; (i) of having, or being filled with, the mindfulness, stillness, calming feeling, and/or beauty created within one's self from simply and fully Just Being from BE-oodling.

BE-oodling

BE-oodling

BE-oodle-ful

My List of ____________________________

____

1 ____________________________

2 ____________________________

3 ____________________________

4 ____________________________

5 ____________________________

6 ____________________________

7 ____________________________

8 ____________________________

9 ____________________________

10 ____________________________

11 ____________________________

MyWi
My Words, My Wisdom

Go ahead, let your wisdom out, your brilliance shine, your soul howl.
Write your own fortune cookie fortune, life mantra, quote, poem, song,
witty one-liner, sarcastic joke…you get the idea. This space - your words, your wisdom:

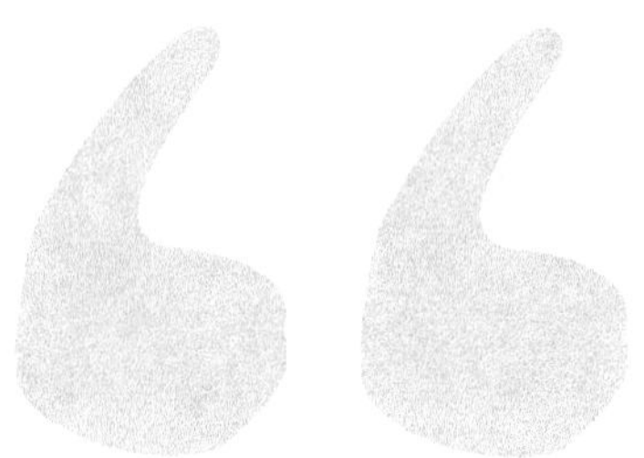

Quotes and poems of others are nice,
Ideas and inspiration abound.
Relying solely on them can be a vice,
For, within myself, the greatest wisdom is found.
- Kerry Raleigh

BE-oodle™

BE-oodle™ – v. to still the mind through absent-minded doodling and allowing one to simply and fully Just Be.

BE-oodle™ – n. the mindfulness, stillness, calming feeling, and/or beauty created within one's self from simply and fully Just Being achieved through BE-oodling.

Other forms: BE-oodling

BE-oodle-ful™ – adj. (i) describing what is created by BE-oodling; (i) of having, or being filled with, the mindfulness, stillness, calming feeling, and/or beauty created within one's self from simply and fully Just Being from BE-oodling.

BE-oodling

BE-oodling

BE-oodle-ful

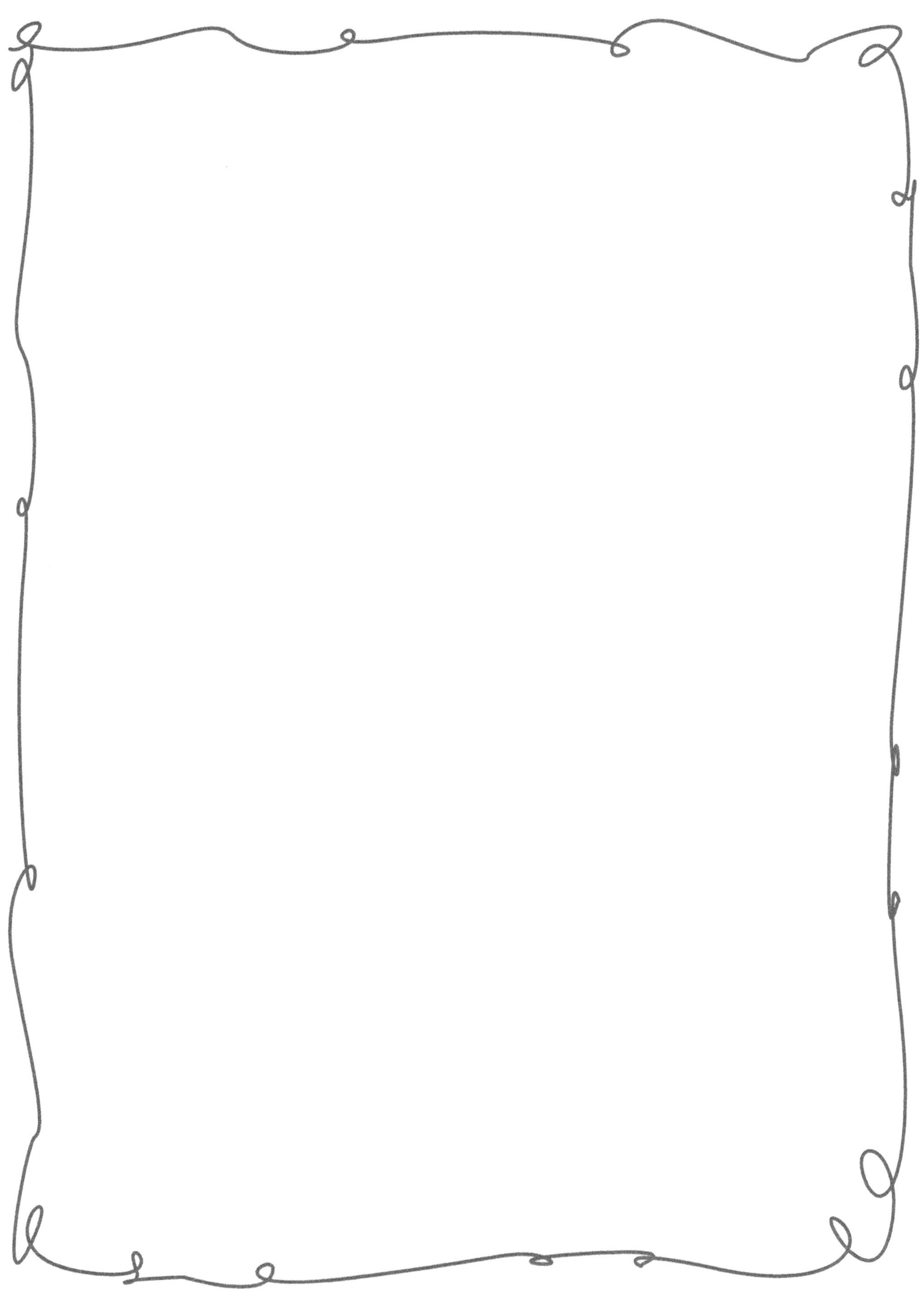

BE-oodle™

BE-oodle™ – v. to still the mind through absent-minded doodling and allowing one to simply and fully Just Be.

BE-oodle™ – n. the mindfulness, stillness, calming feeling, and/or beauty created within one's self from simply and fully Just Being achieved through BE-oodling.

Other forms: BE-oodling

BE-oodle-ful™ – adj. (i) describing what is created by BE-oodling; (i) of having, or being filled with, the mindfulness, stillness, calming feeling, and/or beauty created within one's self from simply and fully Just Being from BE-oodling.

BE-oodling

BE-oodling

BE-oodle-ful

My List of _______________

1 _______________

2 _______________

3 _______________

4 _______________

5 _______________

6 _______________

7 _______________

8 _______________

9 _______________

10 _______________

11 _______________

MyWi
My Words, My Wisdom

Go ahead, let your wisdom out, your brilliance shine, your soul howl.
Write your own fortune cookie fortune, life mantra, quote, poem, song,
witty one-liner, sarcastic joke…you get the idea. This space - your words, your wisdom:

Quotes and poems of others are nice,
Ideas and inspiration abound.
Relying solely on them can be a vice,
For, within myself, the greatest wisdom is found.
- Kerry Raleigh

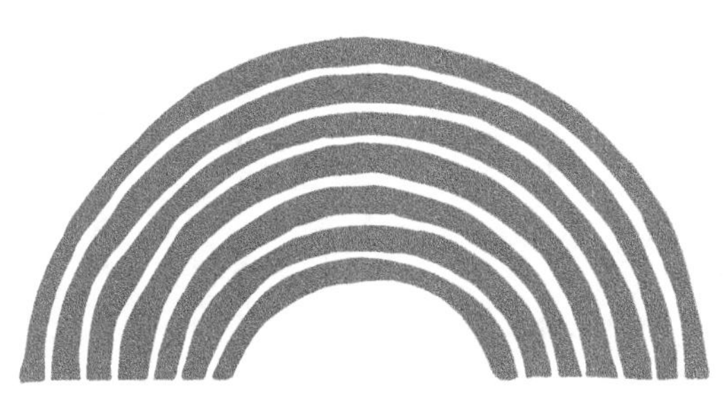

BE-oodle™

BE-oodle™ – v. to still the mind through absent-minded doodling and allowing one to simply and fully Just Be.

BE-oodle™ – n. the mindfulness, stillness, calming feeling, and/or beauty created within one's self from simply and fully Just Being achieved through BE-oodling.

Other forms: BE-oodling

BE-oodle-ful™ – adj. (i) describing what is created by BE-oodling; (i) of having, or being filled with, the mindfulness, stillness, calming feeling, and/or beauty created within one's self from simply and fully Just Being from BE-oodling.

BE-oodling

BE-oodling

BE-oodle-ful

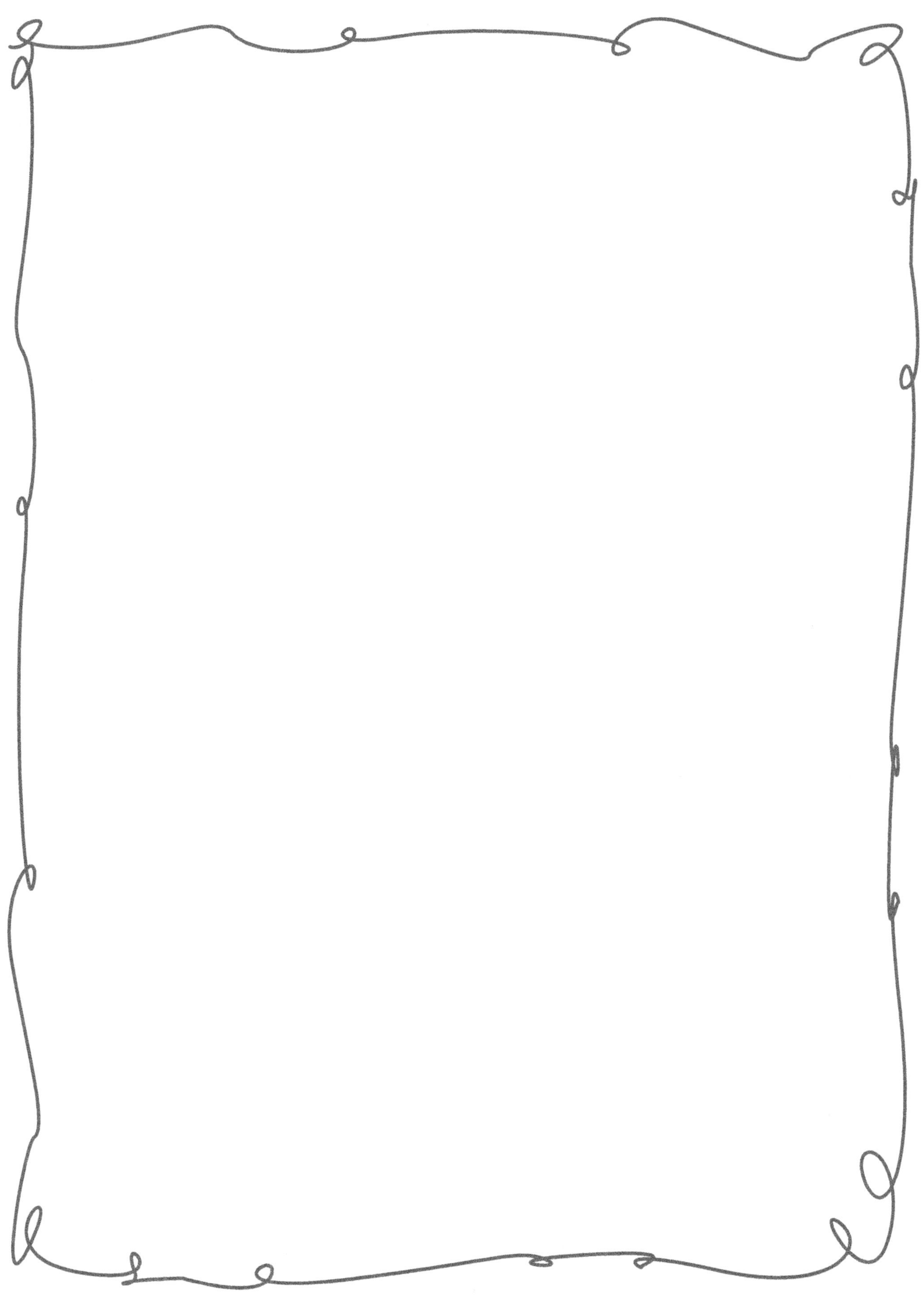

BE-oodle™

BE-oodle™ – v. to still the mind through absent-minded doodling and allowing one to simply and fully Just Be.

BE-oodle™ – n. the mindfulness, stillness, calming feeling, and/or beauty created within one's self from simply and fully Just Being achieved through BE-oodling.

Other forms: BE-oodling

BE-oodle-ful™ – adj. (i) describing what is created by BE-oodling; (i) of having, or being filled with, the mindfulness, stillness, calming feeling, and/or beauty created within one's self from simply and fully Just Being from BE-oodling.

BE-oodling

BE-oodling

BE-oodle-ful

My List of _______________________

1 _______________________

2 _______________________

3 _______________________

4 _______________________

5 _______________________

6 _______________________

7 _______________________

8 _______________________

9 _______________________

10 _______________________

11 _______________________

MyWi
My Words, My Wisdom

Go ahead, let your wisdom out, your brilliance shine, your soul howl.
Write your own fortune cookie fortune, life mantra, quote, poem, song,
witty one-liner, sarcastic joke…you get the idea. This space - your words, your wisdom:

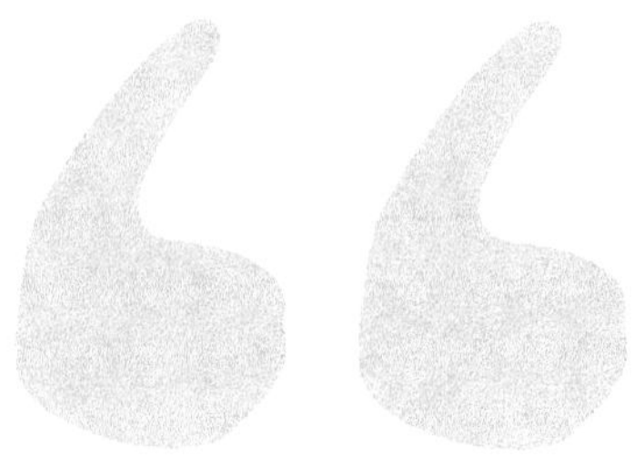

Quotes and poems of others are nice,
Ideas and inspiration abound.
Relying solely on them can be a vice,
For, within myself, the greatest wisdom is found.
- Kerry Raleigh

BE-oodle™

BE-oodle™ – v. to still the mind through absent-minded doodling and allowing one to simply and fully Just Be.

BE-oodle™ – n. the mindfulness, stillness, calming feeling, and/or beauty created within one's self from simply and fully Just Being achieved through BE-oodling.

Other forms: BE-oodling

BE-oodle-ful™ – adj. (i) describing what is created by BE-oodling; (i) of having, or being filled with, the mindfulness, stillness, calming feeling, and/or beauty created within one's self from simply and fully Just Being from BE-oodling.

BE-oodling

BE-oodling

BE-oodle-ful

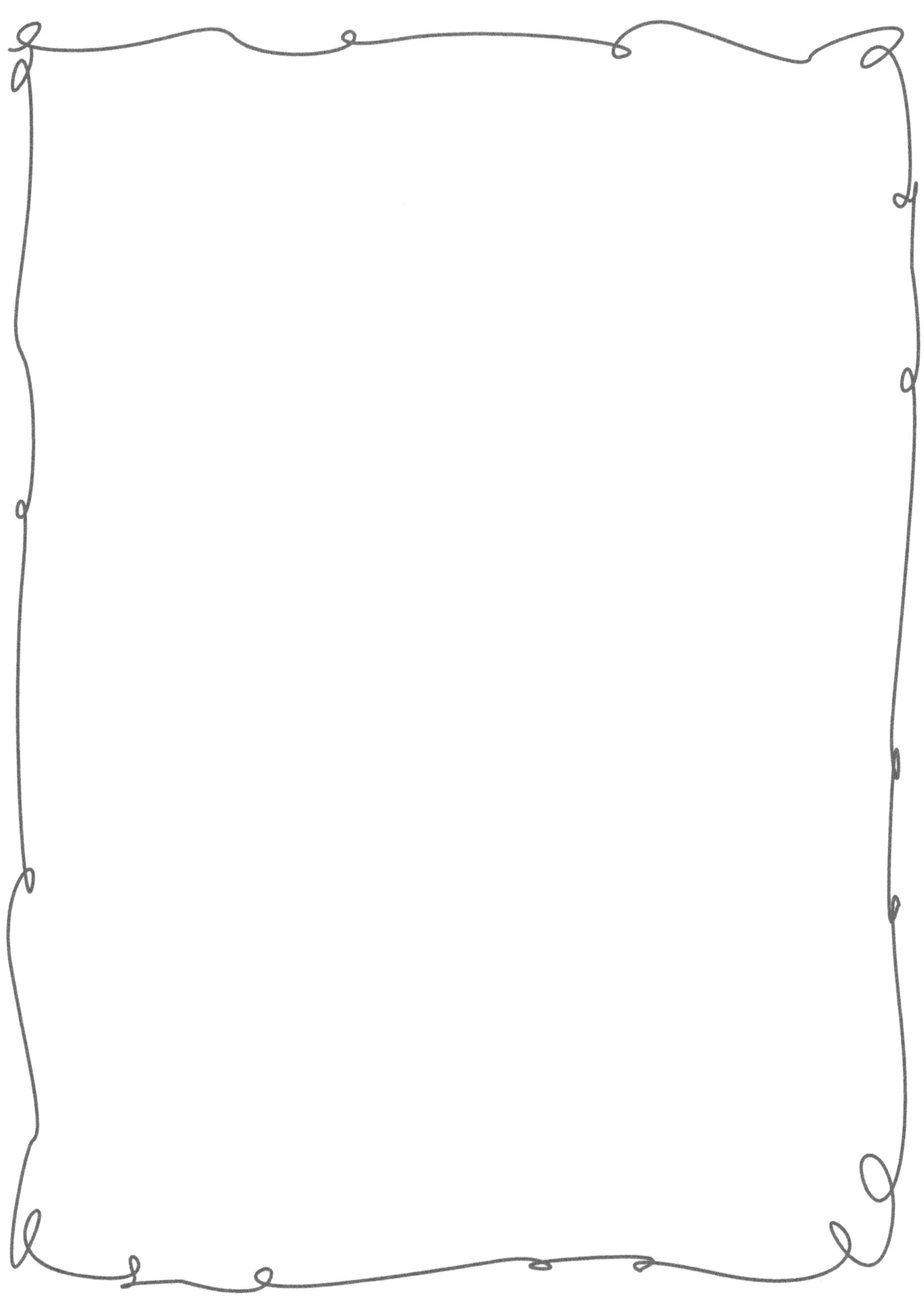

BE-oodle™

BE-oodle™ – v. to still the mind through absent-minded doodling and allowing one to simply and fully Just Be.

BE-oodle™ – n. the mindfulness, stillness, calming feeling, and/or beauty created within one's self from simply and fully Just Being achieved through BE-oodling.

Other forms: BE-oodling

BE-oodle-ful™ – adj. (i) describing what is created by BE-oodling; (i) of having, or being filled with, the mindfulness, stillness, calming feeling, and/or beauty created within one's self from simply and fully Just Being from BE-oodling.

BE-oodling

BE-oodling

BE-oodle-ful

My List of ___________________________

____

1 ___________________________

2 ___________________________

3 ___________________________

4 ___________________________

5 ___________________________

6 ___________________________

7 ___________________________

8 ___________________________

9 ___________________________

10 ___________________________

11 ___________________________

MyWi
My Words, My Wisdom

Go ahead, let your wisdom out, your brilliance shine, your soul howl.
Write your own fortune cookie fortune, life mantra, quote, poem, song,
witty one-liner, sarcastic joke…you get the idea. This space - your words, your wisdom:

Quotes and poems of others are nice,
Ideas and inspiration abound.
Relying solely on them can be a vice,
For, within myself, the greatest wisdom is found.
- Kerry Raleigh

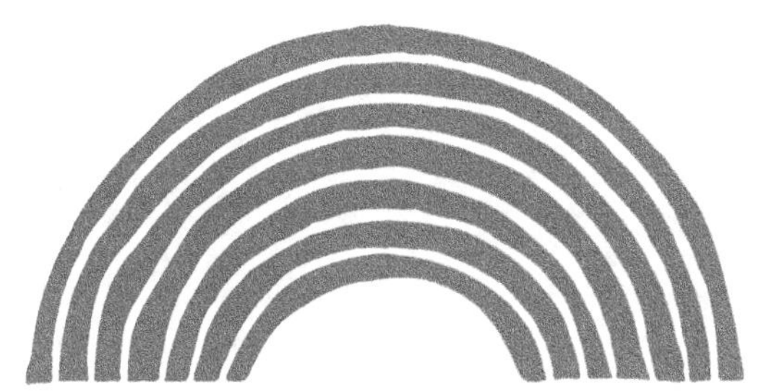

BE-oodle™

BE-oodle™ – v. to still the mind through absent-minded doodling and allowing one to simply and fully Just Be.

BE-oodle™ – n. the mindfulness, stillness, calming feeling, and/or beauty created within one's self from simply and fully Just Being achieved through BE-oodling.

Other forms: BE-oodling

BE-oodle-ful™ – adj. (i) describing what is created by BE-oodling; (i) of having, or being filled with, the mindfulness, stillness, calming feeling, and/or beauty created within one's self from simply and fully Just Being from BE-oodling.

BE-oodling

BE-oodling

BE-oodle-ful

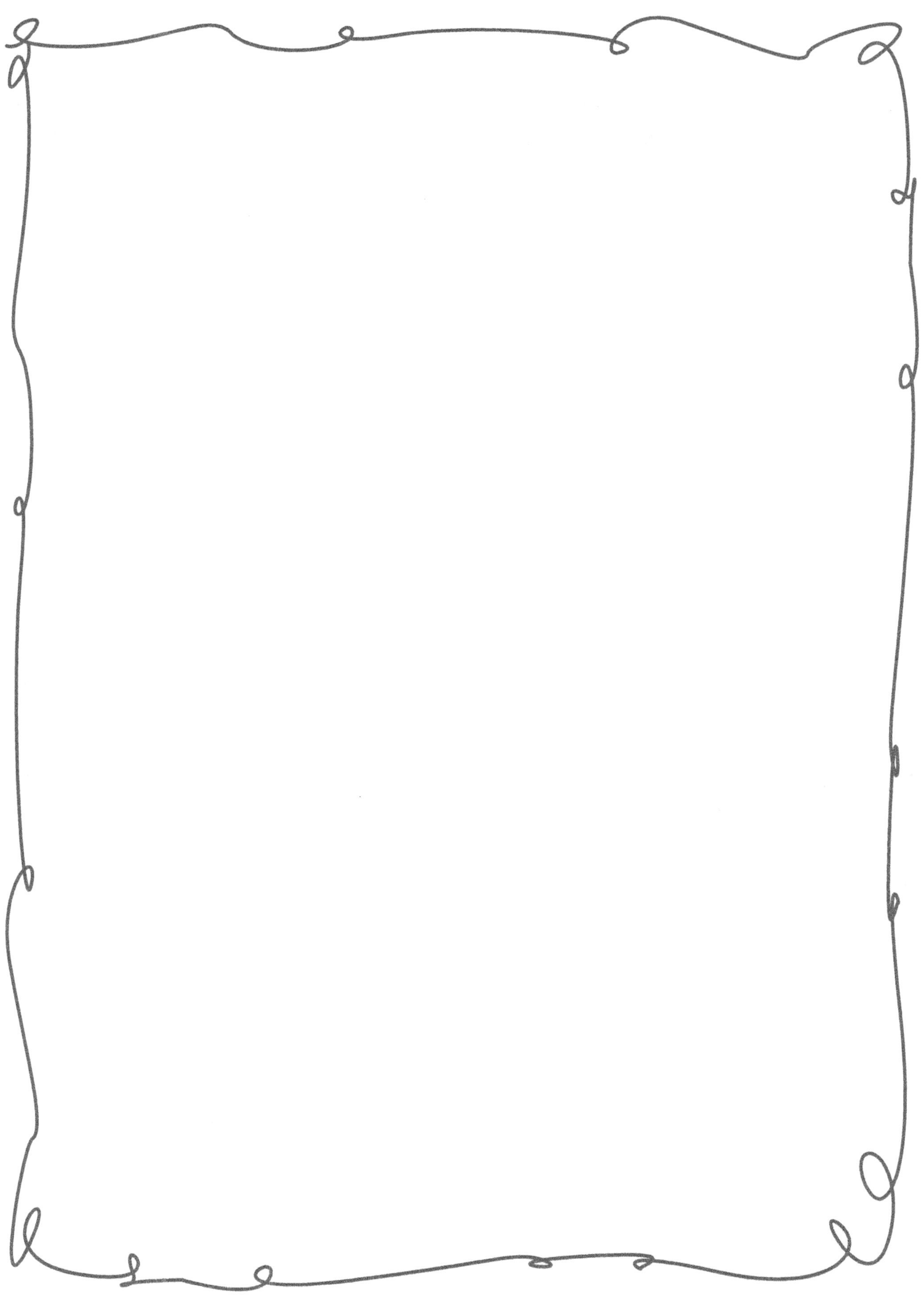

BE-oodle™

BE-oodle™ – v. to still the mind through absent-minded doodling and allowing one to simply and fully Just Be.

BE-oodle™ – n. the mindfulness, stillness, calming feeling, and/or beauty created within one's self from simply and fully Just Being achieved through BE-oodling.

Other forms: BE-oodling

BE-oodle-ful™ – adj. (i) describing what is created by BE-oodling; (i) of having, or being filled with, the mindfulness, stillness, calming feeling, and/or beauty created within one's self from simply and fully Just Being from BE-oodling.

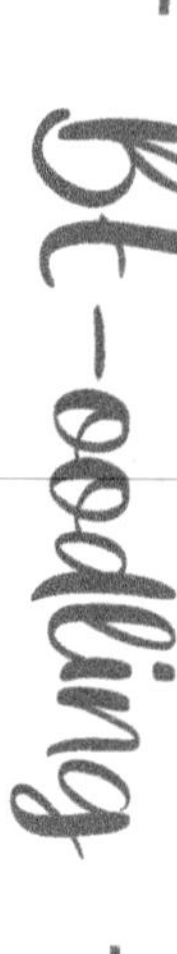

BE-oodling

BE-oodling

BE-oodle-ful

My List of _______________

1 _______________

2 _______________

3 _______________

4 _______________

5 _______________

6 _______________

7 _______________

8 _______________

9 _______________

10 _______________

11 _______________

MyWi
My Words, My Wisdom

Go ahead, let your wisdom out, your brilliance shine, your soul howl.
Write your own fortune cookie fortune, life mantra, quote, poem, song,
witty one-liner, sarcastic joke…you get the idea. This space - your words, your wisdom:

Quotes and poems of others are nice,
Ideas and inspiration abound.
Relying solely on them can be a vice,
For, within myself, the greatest wisdom is found.
- Kerry Raleigh

BE-oodle™

BE-oodle™ – v. to still the mind through absent-minded doodling and allowing one to simply and fully Just Be.

BE-oodle™ – n. the mindfulness, stillness, calming feeling, and/or beauty created within one's self from simply and fully Just Being achieved through BE-oodling.

Other forms: BE-oodling

BE-oodle-ful™ – adj. (i) describing what is created by BE-oodling; (i) of having, or being filled with, the mindfulness, stillness, calming feeling, and/or beauty created within one's self from simply and fully Just Being from BE-oodling.

BE-oodling

BE-oodling

BE-oodle-ful

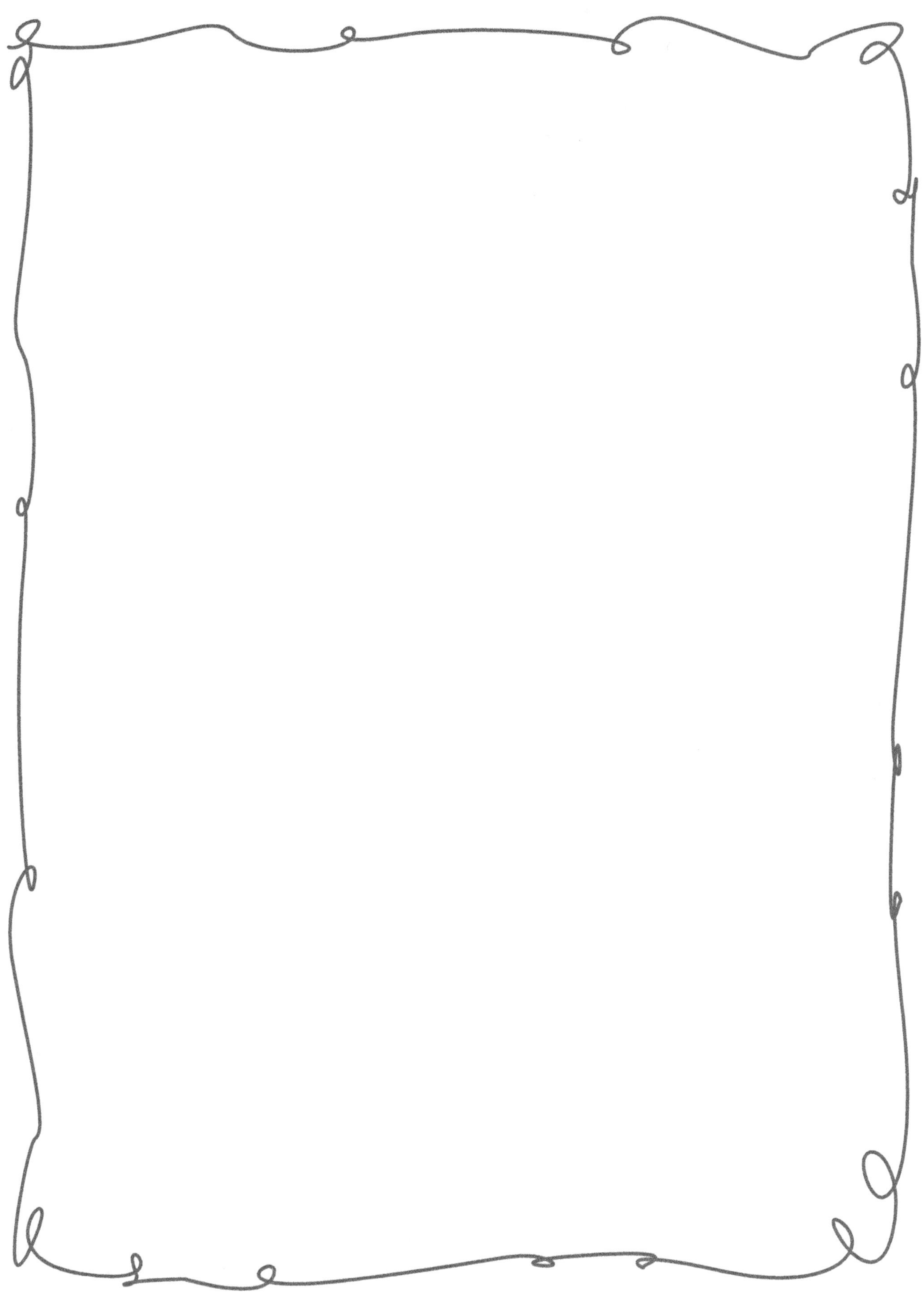

BE-oodle™

BE-oodle™ – v. to still the mind through absent-minded doodling and allowing one to simply and fully Just Be.

BE-oodle™ – n. the mindfulness, stillness, calming feeling, and/or beauty created within one's self from simply and fully Just Being achieved through BE-oodling.

Other forms: BE-oodling

BE-oodle-ful™ – adj. (i) describing what is created by BE-oodling; (i) of having, or being filled with, the mindfulness, stillness, calming feeling, and/or beauty created within one's self from simply and fully Just Being from BE-oodling.

BE-oodling

BE-oodling

BE-oodle-ful

My List of ___________________________

____

1 ______________________________

2 ______________________________

3 ______________________________

4 ______________________________

5 ______________________________

6 ______________________________

7 ______________________________

8 ______________________________

9 ______________________________

10 ______________________________

11 ______________________________

MyWi
My Words, My Wisdom

Go ahead, let your wisdom out, your brilliance shine, your soul howl.
Write your own fortune cookie fortune, life mantra, quote, poem, song,
witty one-liner, sarcastic joke…you get the idea. This space - your words, your wisdom:

Quotes and poems of others are nice,
Ideas and inspiration abound.
Relying solely on them can be a vice,
For, within myself, the greatest wisdom is found.
- Kerry Raleigh

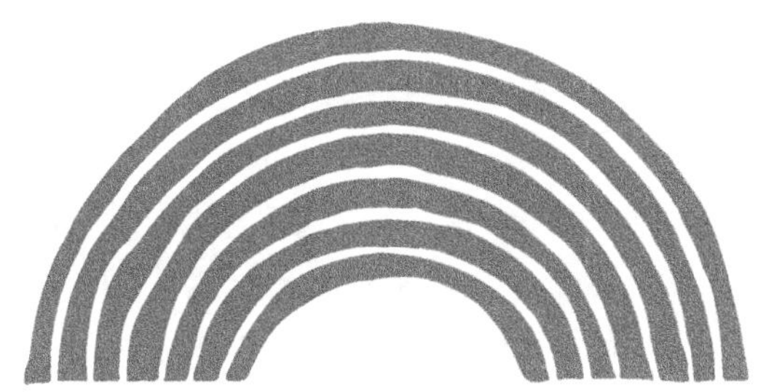

BE-oodle™

BE-oodle™ – v. to still the mind through absent-minded doodling and allowing one to simply and fully Just Be.

BE-oodle™ – n. the mindfulness, stillness, calming feeling, and/or beauty created within one's self from simply and fully Just Being achieved through BE-oodling.

Other forms: BE-oodling

BE-oodle-ful™ – adj. (i) describing what is created by BE-oodling; (i) of having, or being filled with, the mindfulness, stillness, calming feeling, and/or beauty created within one's self from simply and fully Just Being from BE-oodling.

BE-oodling

BE-oodling

BE-oodle-ful

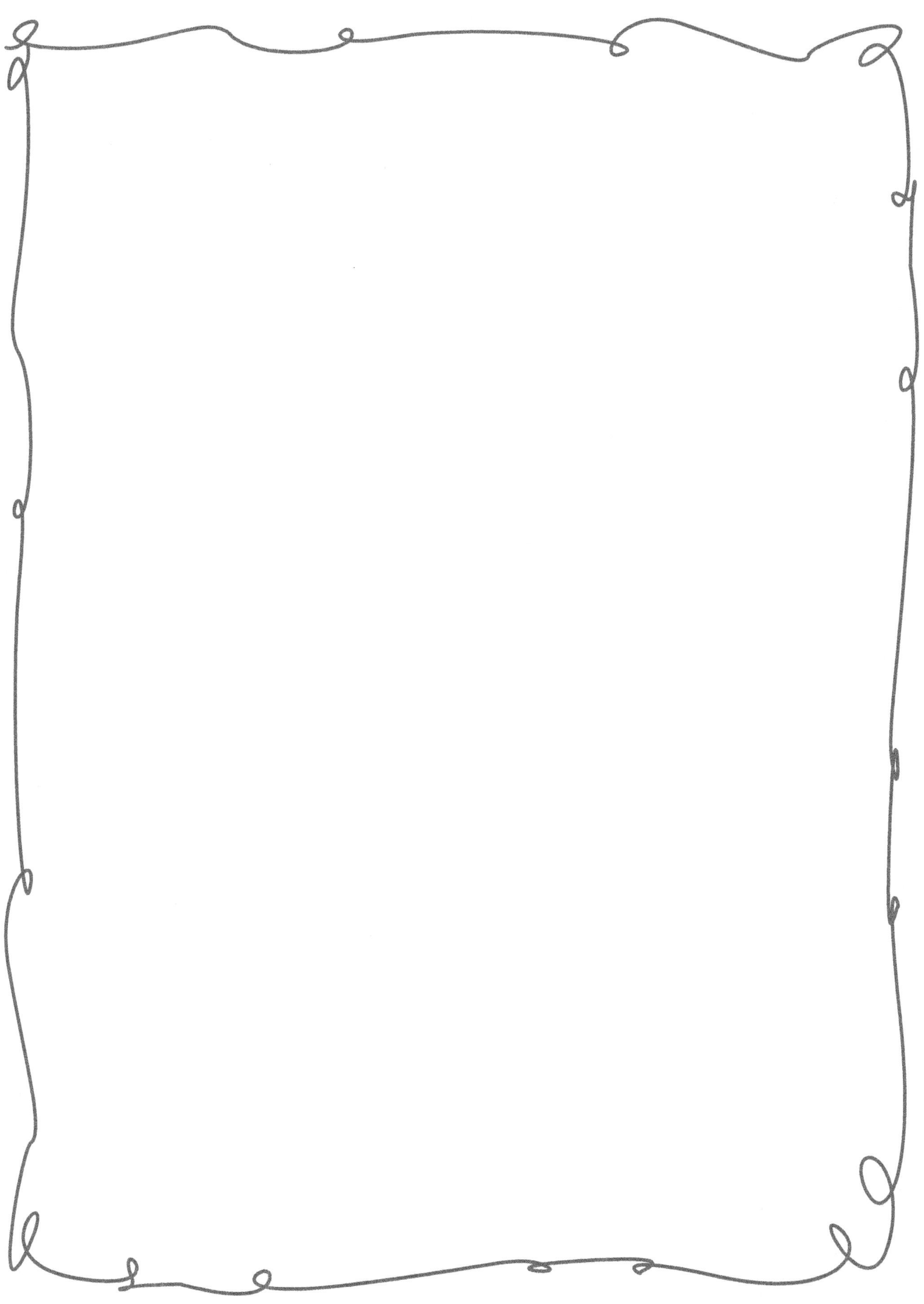

BE-oodle™

BE-oodle™ – v. to still the mind through absent-minded doodling and allowing one to simply and fully Just Be.

BE-oodle™ – n. the mindfulness, stillness, calming feeling, and/or beauty created within one's self from simply and fully Just Being achieved through BE-oodling.

Other forms: BE-oodling

BE-oodle-ful™ – adj. (i) describing what is created by BE-oodling; (i) of having, or being filled with, the mindfulness, stillness, calming feeling, and/or beauty created within one's self from simply and fully Just Being from BE-oodling.

BE-oodle-ful

My List of ___________________

____

1 ___________________

2 ___________________

3 ___________________

4 ___________________

5 ___________________

6 ___________________

7 ___________________

8 ___________________

9 ___________________

10 ___________________

11 ___________________

MyWi
My Words, My Wisdom

Go ahead, let your wisdom out, your brilliance shine, your soul howl.
Write your own fortune cookie fortune, life mantra, quote, poem, song,
witty one-liner, sarcastic joke…you get the idea. This space - your words, your wisdom:

Quotes and poems of others are nice,
Ideas and inspiration abound.
Relying solely on them can be a vice,
For, within myself, the greatest wisdom is found.
- Kerry Raleigh

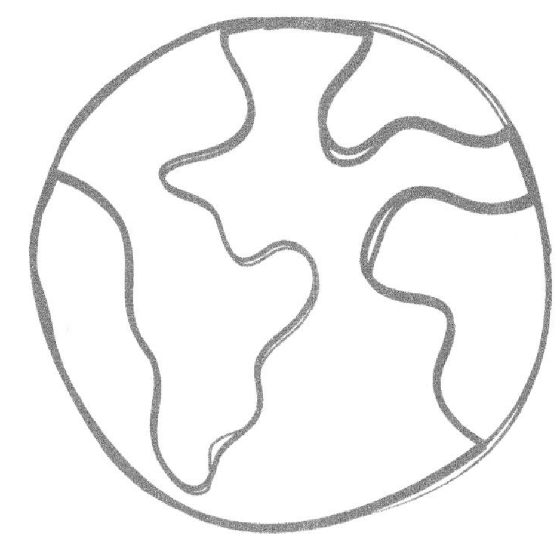

BE-oodle™

BE-oodle™ – v. to still the mind through absent-minded doodling and allowing one to simply and fully Just Be.

BE-oodle™ – n. the mindfulness, stillness, calming feeling, and/or beauty created within one's self from simply and fully Just Being achieved through BE-oodling.

Other forms: BE-oodling

BE-oodle-ful™ – adj. (i) describing what is created by BE-oodling; (i) of having, or being filled with, the mindfulness, stillness, calming feeling, and/or beauty created within one's self from simply and fully Just Being from BE-oodling.

BE-oodling

BE-oodling

BE-oodle-ful

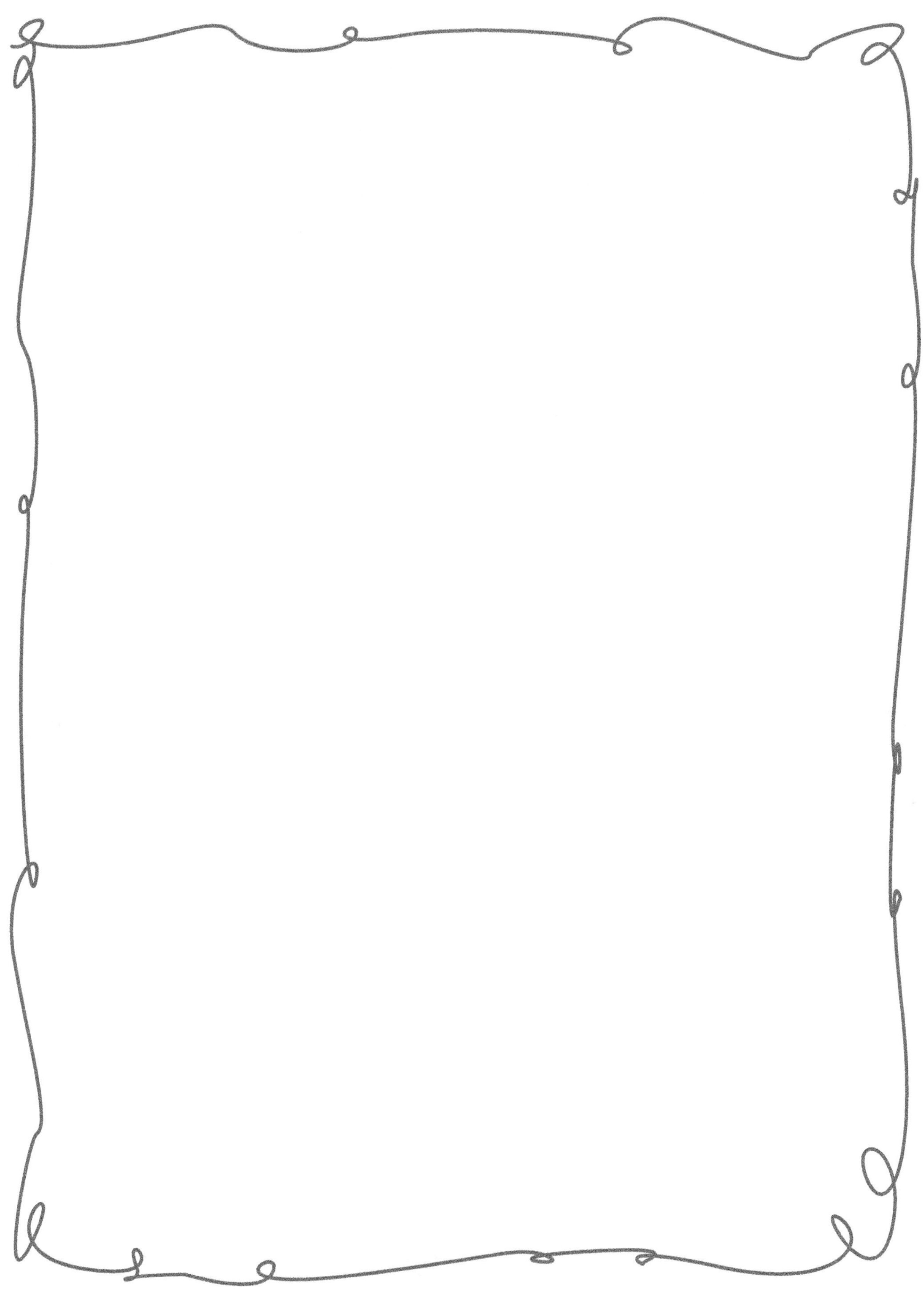

BE-oodle™

BE-oodle™ – v. to still the mind through absent-minded doodling and allowing one to simply and fully Just Be.

BE-oodle™ – n. the mindfulness, stillness, calming feeling, and/or beauty created within one's self from simply and fully Just Being achieved through BE-oodling.

Other forms: BE-oodling

BE-oodle-ful™ – adj. (i) describing what is created by BE-oodling; (i) of having, or being filled with, the mindfulness, stillness, calming feeling, and/or beauty created within one's self from simply and fully Just Being from BE-oodling.

BE-oodling

BE-oodling

BE-oodle-ful

My List of ___________________

____

1 ___________________

2 ___________________

3 ___________________

4 ___________________

5 ___________________

6 ___________________

7 ___________________

8 ___________________

9 ___________________

10 ___________________

11 ___________________

MyWi
My Words, My Wisdom

Go ahead, let your wisdom out, your brilliance shine, your soul howl.
Write your own fortune cookie fortune, life mantra, quote, poem, song,
witty one-liner, sarcastic joke…you get the idea. This space - your words, your wisdom:

Quotes and poems of others are nice,
Ideas and inspiration abound.
Relying solely on them can be a vice,
For, within myself, the greatest wisdom is found.
- Kerry Raleigh

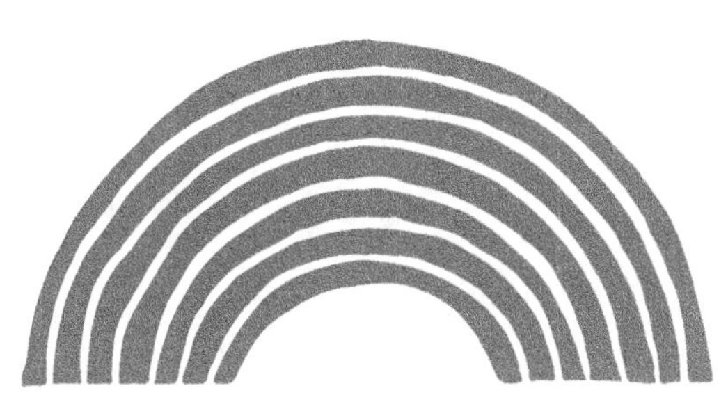

BE-oodle™

BE-oodle™ – v. to still the mind through absent-minded doodling and allowing one to simply and fully Just Be.

BE-oodle™ – n. the mindfulness, stillness, calming feeling, and/or beauty created within one's self from simply and fully Just Being achieved through BE-oodling.

Other forms: BE-oodling

BE-oodle-ful™ – adj. (i) describing what is created by BE-oodling; (i) of having, or being filled with, the mindfulness, stillness, calming feeling, and/or beauty created within one's self from simply and fully Just Being from BE-oodling.

BE-oodling

BE-oodling

BE-oodle-ful

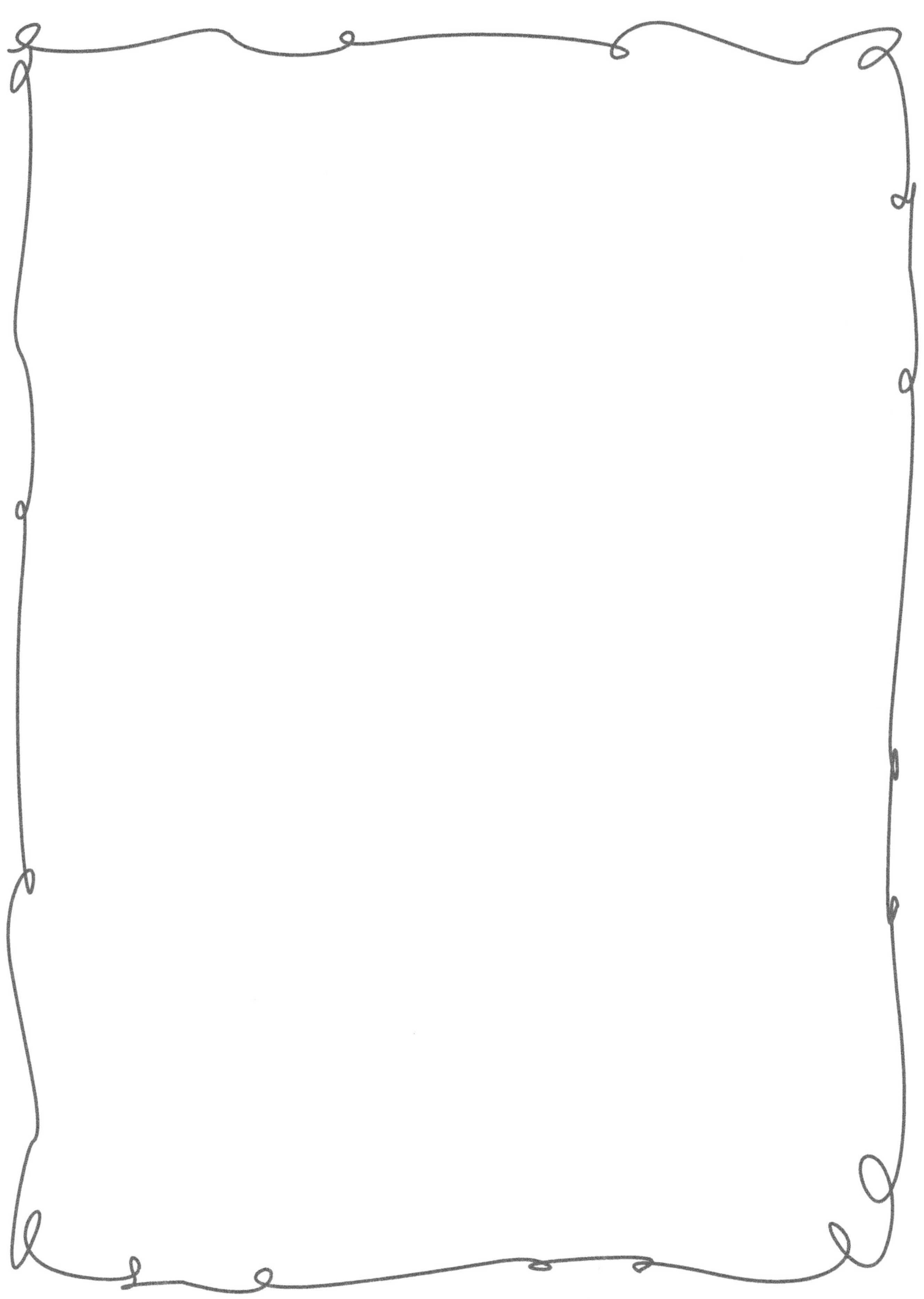

BE-oodle™

BE-oodle™ – v. to still the mind through absent-minded doodling and allowing one to simply and fully Just Be.

BE-oodle™ – n. the mindfulness, stillness, calming feeling, and/or beauty created within one's self from simply and fully Just Being achieved through BE-oodling.

Other forms: BE-oodling

BE-oodle-ful™ – adj. (i) describing what is created by BE-oodling; (i) of having, or being filled with, the mindfulness, stillness, calming feeling, and/or beauty created within one's self from simply and fully Just Being from BE-oodling.

BE-oodling

BE-oodling

BE-oodle-ful

My List of _______________

____

1 _______________________________

2 _______________________________

3 _______________________________

4 _______________________________

5 _______________________________

6 _______________________________

7 _______________________________

8 _______________________________

9 _______________________________

10 _______________________________

11 _______________________________

MyWi
My Words, My Wisdom

Go ahead, let your wisdom out, your brilliance shine, your soul howl.
Write your own fortune cookie fortune, life mantra, quote, poem, song,
witty one-liner, sarcastic joke…you get the idea. This space - your words, your wisdom:

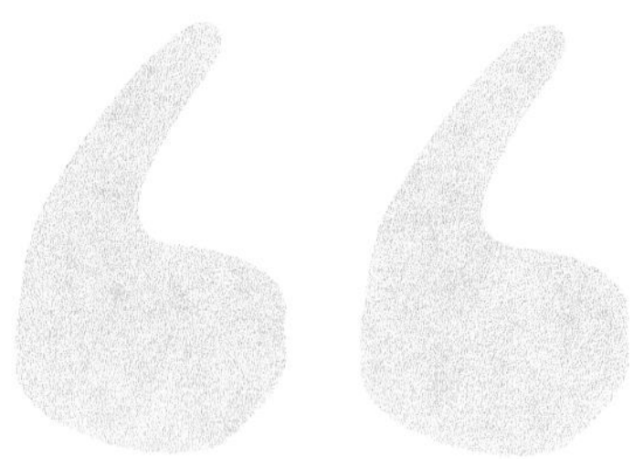

Quotes and poems of others are nice,
Ideas and inspiration abound.
Relying solely on them can be a vice,
For, within myself, the greatest wisdom is found.
- Kerry Raleigh

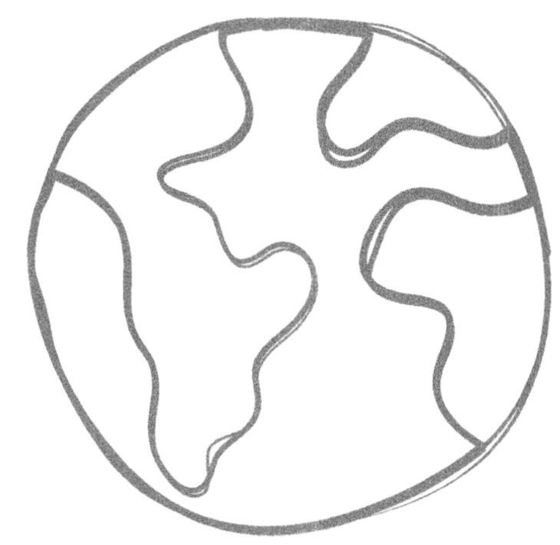

BE-oodle™

BE-oodle™ – v. to still the mind through absent-minded doodling and allowing one to simply and fully Just Be.

BE-oodle™ – n. the mindfulness, stillness, calming feeling, and/or beauty created within one's self from simply and fully Just Being achieved through BE-oodling.

Other forms: BE-oodling

BE-oodle-ful™ – adj. (i) describing what is created by BE-oodling; (i) of having, or being filled with, the mindfulness, stillness, calming feeling, and/or beauty created within one's self from simply and fully Just Being from BE-oodling.

BE-oodling

BE-oodling

BE-oodle-ful

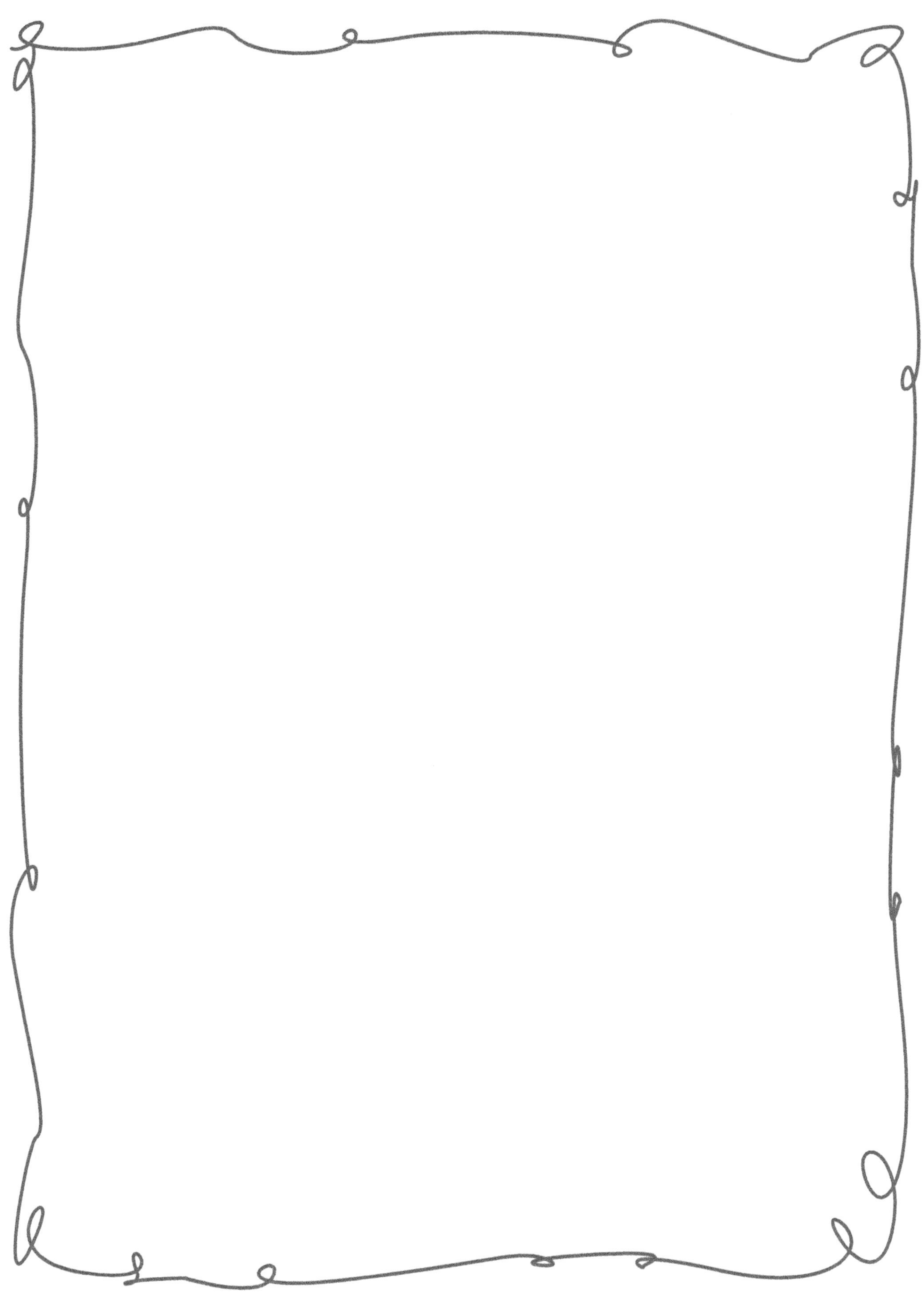

BE-oodle™

BE-oodle™ – v. to still the mind through absent-minded doodling and allowing one to simply and fully Just Be.

BE-oodle™ – n. the mindfulness, stillness, calming feeling, and/or beauty created within one's self from simply and fully Just Being achieved through BE-oodling.

Other forms: BE-oodling

BE-oodle-ful™ – adj. (i) describing what is created by BE-oodling; (i) of having, or being filled with, the mindfulness, stillness, calming feeling, and/or beauty created within one's self from simply and fully Just Being from BE-oodling.

BE-oodling

BE-oodling

BE-oodle-ful

My List of _______________

1 ______________________________

2 ______________________________

3 ______________________________

4 ______________________________

5 ______________________________

6 ______________________________

7 ______________________________

8 ______________________________

9 ______________________________

10 ______________________________

11 ______________________________

Go ahead, let your wisdom out, your brilliance shine, your soul howl.
Write your own fortune cookie fortune, life mantra, quote, poem, song,
witty one-liner, sarcastic joke…you get the idea. This space - your words, your wisdom:

Quotes and poems of others are nice,
Ideas and inspiration abound.
Relying solely on them can be a vice,
For, within myself, the greatest wisdom is found.
- Kerry Raleigh

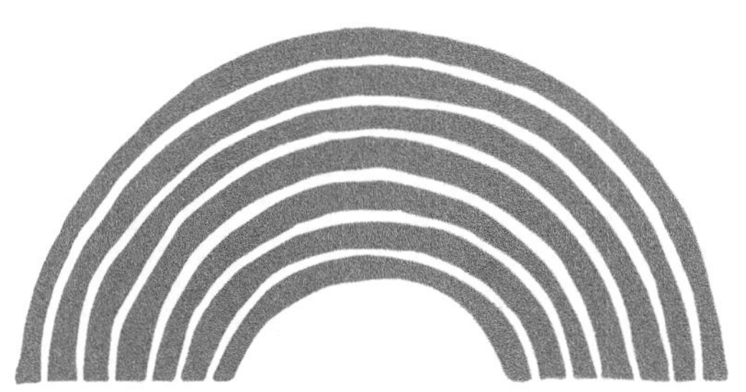

BE-oodle™

BE-oodle™ – v. to still the mind through absent-minded doodling and allowing one to simply and fully Just Be.

BE-oodle™ – n. the mindfulness, stillness, calming feeling, and/or beauty created within one's self from simply and fully Just Being achieved through BE-oodling.

Other forms: BE-oodling

BE-oodle-ful™ – adj. (i) describing what is created by BE-oodling; (i) of having, or being filled with, the mindfulness, stillness, calming feeling, and/or beauty created within one's self from simply and fully Just Being from BE-oodling.

BE-oodling

BE-oodling

BE-oodle-ful

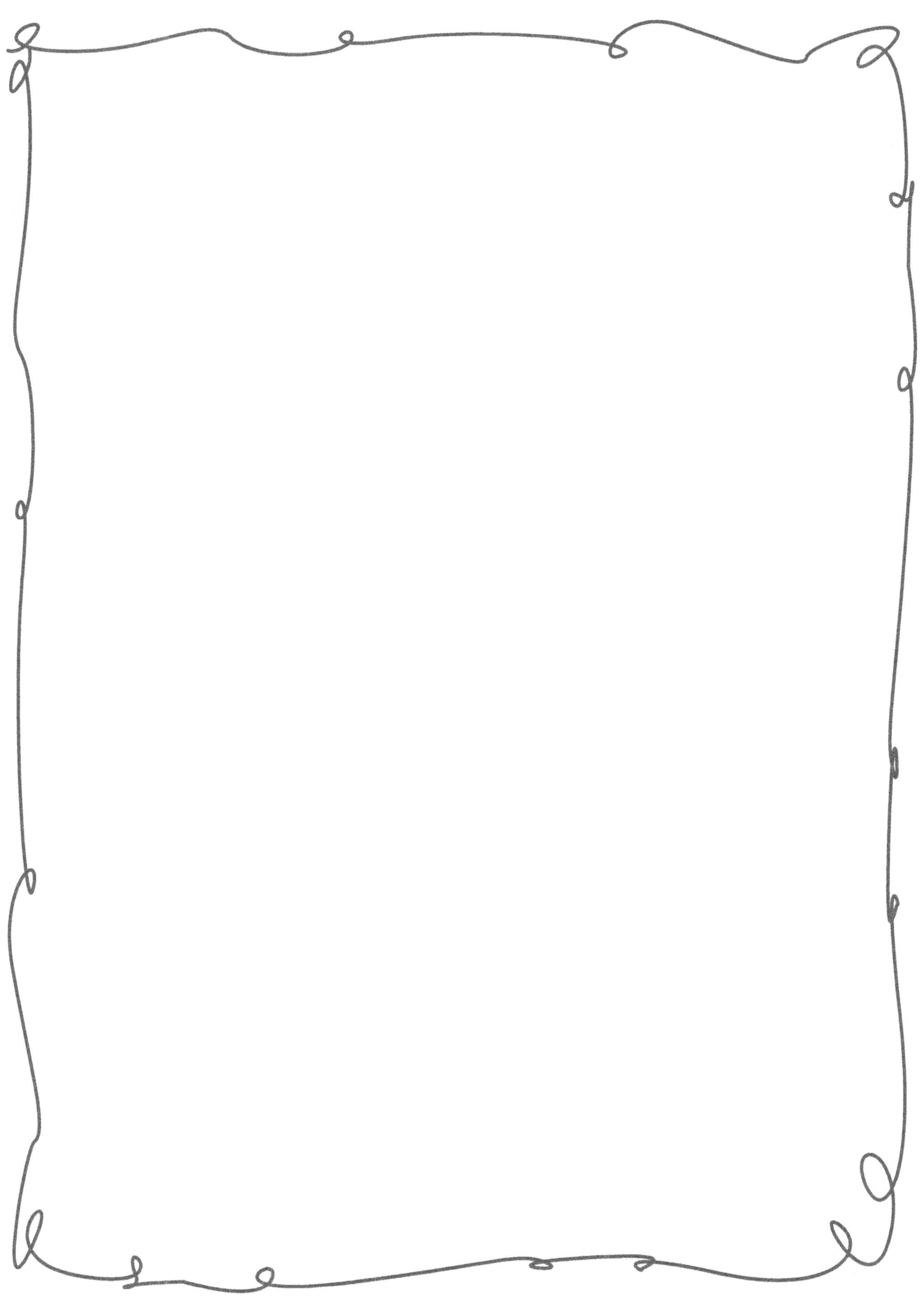

BE-oodle™

BE-oodle™ – v. to still the mind through absent-minded doodling and allowing one to simply and fully Just Be.

BE-oodle™ – n. the mindfulness, stillness, calming feeling, and/or beauty created within one's self from simply and fully Just Being achieved through BE-oodling.

Other forms: BE-oodling

BE-oodle-ful™ – adj. (i) describing what is created by BE-oodling; (i) of having, or being filled with, the mindfulness, stillness, calming feeling, and/or beauty created within one's self from simply and fully Just Being from BE-oodling.

BE-oodling

BE-oodling

BE-oodle-ful

My List of _______________________

1 _______________________

2 _______________________

3 _______________________

4 _______________________

5 _______________________

6 _______________________

7 _______________________

8 _______________________

9 _______________________

10 _______________________

11 _______________________

MyWi
My Words, My Wisdom

Go ahead, let your wisdom out, your brilliance shine, your soul howl.
Write your own fortune cookie fortune, life mantra, quote, poem, song,
witty one-liner, sarcastic joke…you get the idea. This space - your words, your wisdom:

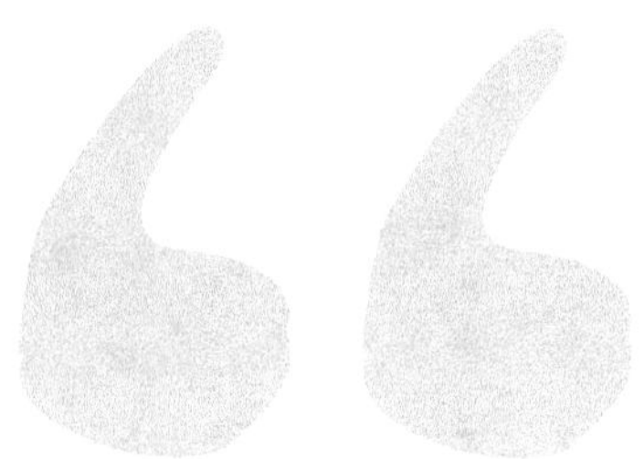

Quotes and poems of others are nice,
Ideas and inspiration abound.
Relying solely on them can be a vice,
For, within myself, the greatest wisdom is found.
- Kerry Raleigh

BE-oodle™

BE-oodle™ – v. to still the mind through absent-minded doodling and allowing one to simply and fully Just Be.

BE-oodle™ – n. the mindfulness, stillness, calming feeling, and/or beauty created within one's self from simply and fully Just Being achieved through BE-oodling.

Other forms: BE-oodling

BE-oodle-ful™ – adj. (i) describing what is created by BE-oodling; (i) of having, or being filled with, the mindfulness, stillness, calming feeling, and/or beauty created within one's self from simply and fully Just Being from BE-oodling.

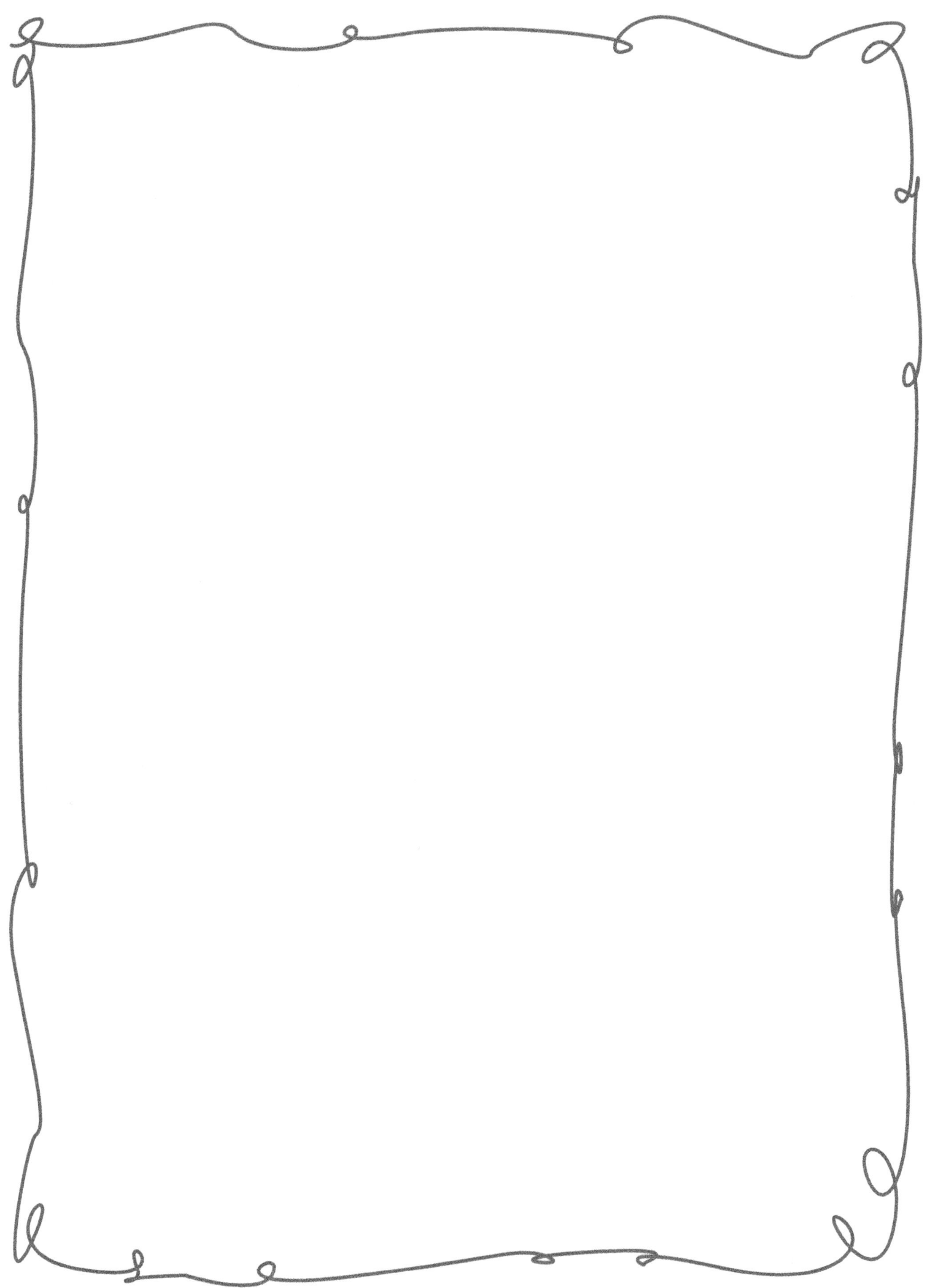

BE-oodle™

BE-oodle™ – v. to still the mind through absent-minded doodling and allowing one to simply and fully Just Be.

BE-oodle™ – n. the mindfulness, stillness, calming feeling, and/or beauty created within one's self from simply and fully Just Being achieved through BE-oodling.

Other forms: BE-oodling

BE-oodle-ful™ – adj. (i) describing what is created by BE-oodling; (i) of having, or being filled with, the mindfulness, stillness, calming feeling, and/or beauty created within one's self from simply and fully Just Being from BE-oodling.

BE-oodling

BE-oodling

BE-oodle-ful

My List of _______________

1 _______________

2 _______________

3 _______________

4 _______________

5 _______________

6 _______________

7 _______________

8 _______________

9 _______________

10 _______________

11 _______________

MyWi
My Words, My Wisdom

Go ahead, let your wisdom out, your brilliance shine, your soul howl.
Write your own fortune cookie fortune, life mantra, quote, poem, song,
witty one-liner, sarcastic joke…you get the idea. This space - your words, your wisdom:

Quotes and poems of others are nice,
Ideas and inspiration abound.
Relying solely on them can be a vice,
For, within myself, the greatest wisdom is found.
- Kerry Raleigh

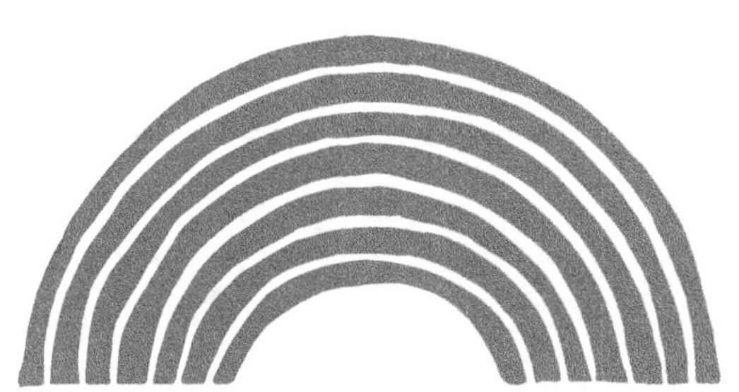

BE-oodle™

BE-oodle™ – v. to still the mind through absent-minded doodling and allowing one to simply and fully Just Be.

BE-oodle™ – n. the mindfulness, stillness, calming feeling, and/or beauty created within one's self from simply and fully Just Being achieved through BE-oodling.

Other forms: BE-oodling

BE-oodle-ful™ – adj. (i) describing what is created by BE-oodling; (i) of having, or being filled with, the mindfulness, stillness, calming feeling, and/or beauty created within one's self from simply and fully Just Being from BE-oodling.

BE-oodling

BE-oodling

BE-oodle-ful

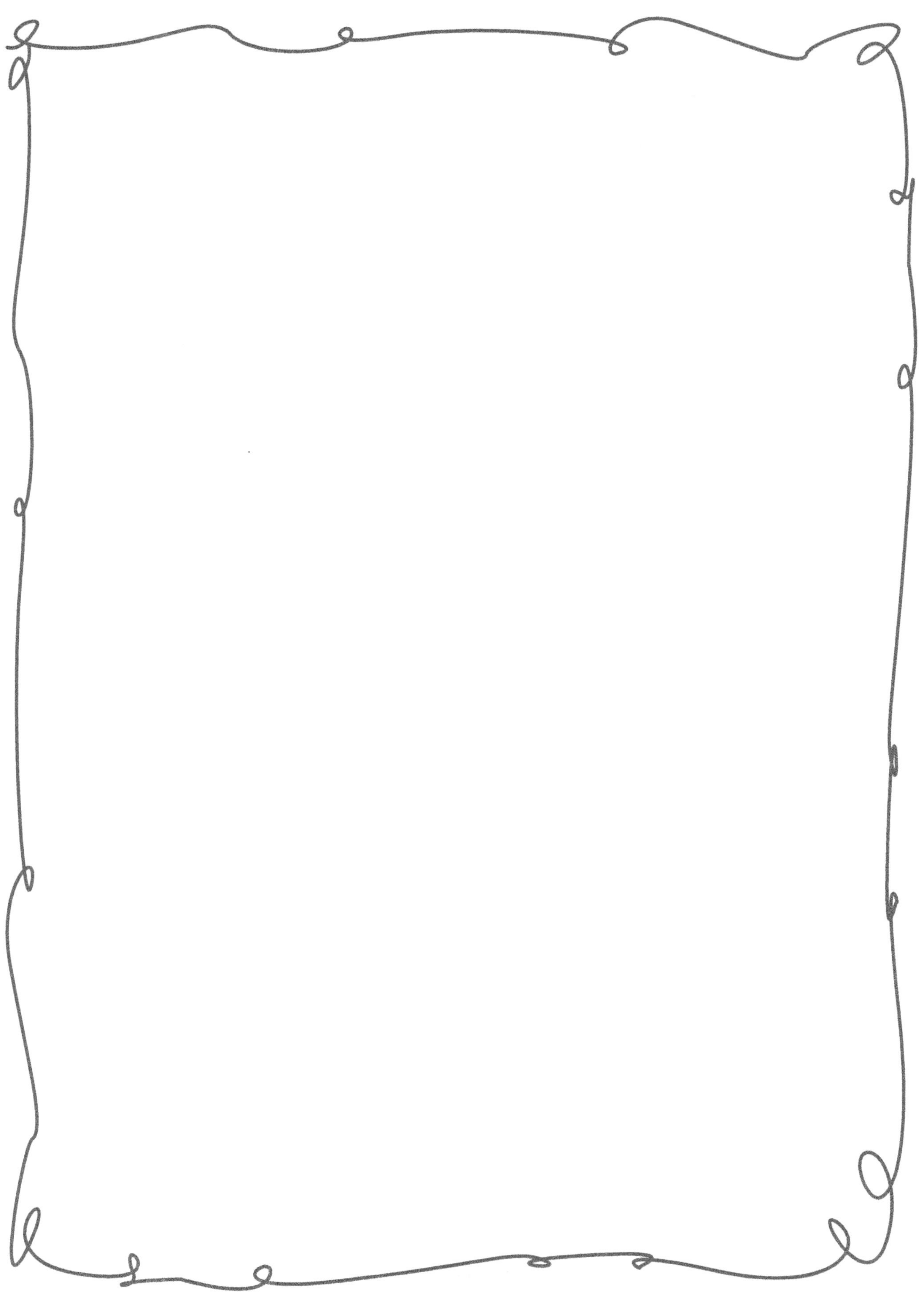

BE-oodle™

BE-oodle™ – v. to still the mind through absent-minded doodling and allowing one to simply and fully Just Be.

BE-oodle™ – n. the mindfulness, stillness, calming feeling, and/or beauty created within one's self from simply and fully Just Being achieved through BE-oodling.

Other forms: BE-oodling

BE-oodle-ful™ – adj. (i) describing what is created by BE-oodling; (i) of having, or being filled with, the mindfulness, stillness, calming feeling, and/or beauty created within one's self from simply and fully Just Being from BE-oodling.

BE-oodling

BE-oodling

BE-oodle-ful

My List of ______________________________

1 ______________________________

2 ______________________________

3 ______________________________

4 ______________________________

5 ______________________________

6 ______________________________

7 ______________________________

8 ______________________________

9 ______________________________

10 ______________________________

11 ______________________________

MyWi
My Words, My Wisdom

Go ahead, let your wisdom out, your brilliance shine, your soul howl.
Write your own fortune cookie fortune, life mantra, quote, poem, song,
witty one-liner, sarcastic joke…you get the idea. This space - your words, your wisdom:

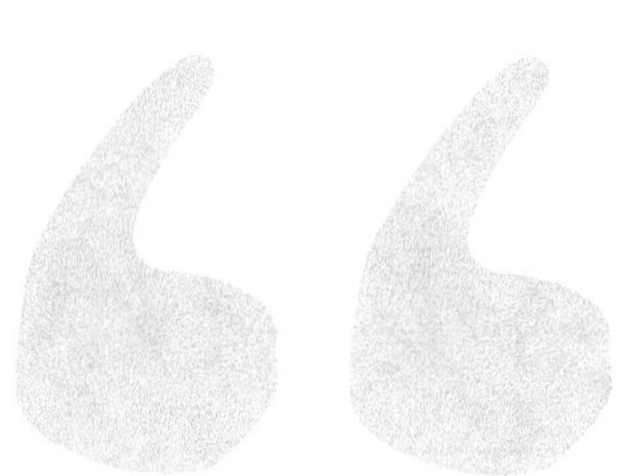

Quotes and poems of others are nice,
Ideas and inspiration abound.
Relying solely on them can be a vice,
For, within myself, the greatest wisdom is found.
- Kerry Raleigh

BE-oodle™

BE-oodle™ – v. to still the mind through absent-minded doodling and allowing one to simply and fully Just Be.

BE-oodle™ – n. the mindfulness, stillness, calming feeling, and/or beauty created within one's self from simply and fully Just Being achieved through BE-oodling.

Other forms: BE-oodling

BE-oodle-ful™ – adj. (i) describing what is created by BE-oodling; (i) of having, or being filled with, the mindfulness, stillness, calming feeling, and/or beauty created within one's self from simply and fully Just Being from BE-oodling.

BE-oodling

BE-oodling

BE-oodle-ful

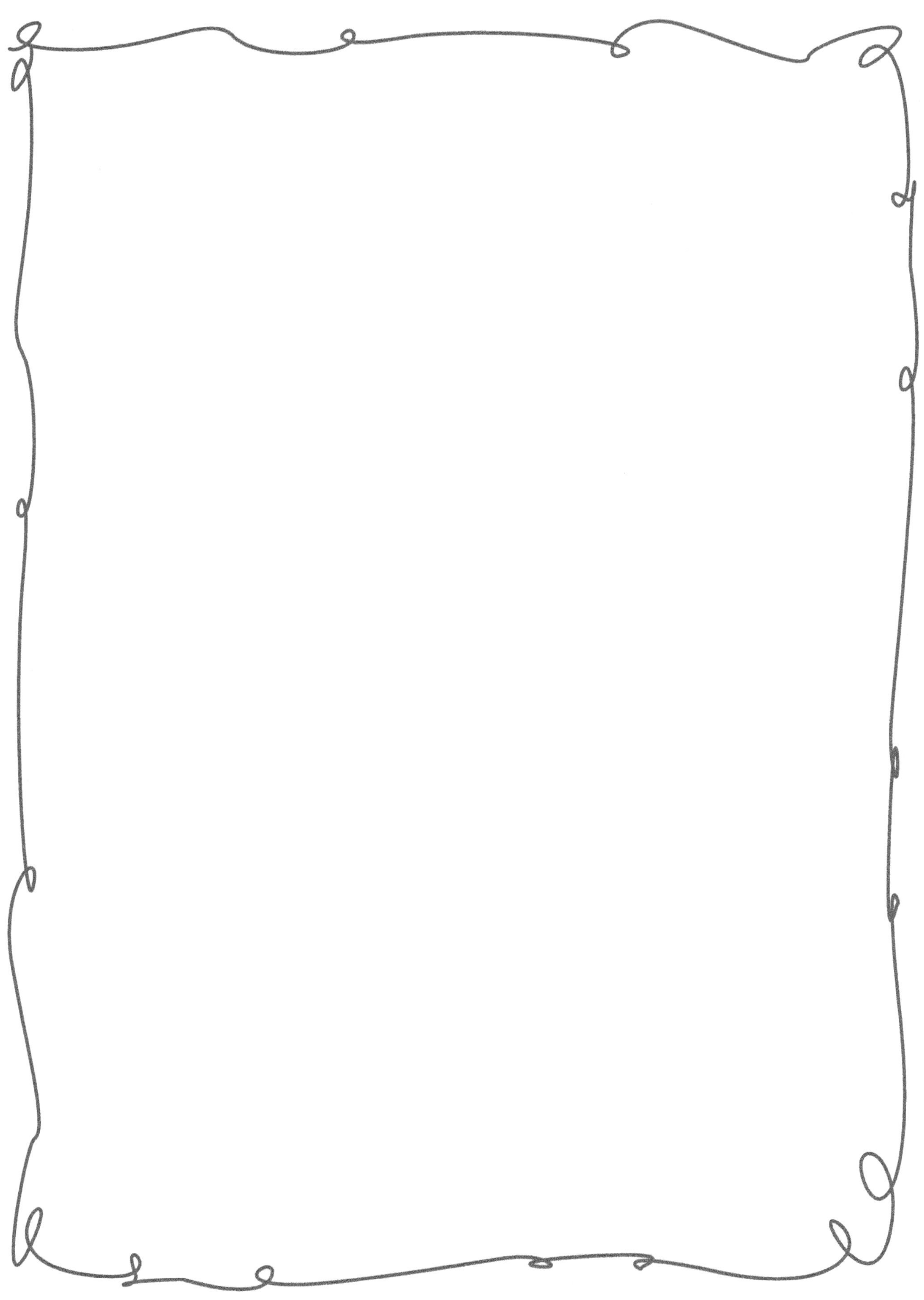

BE-oodle™

BE-oodle™ – v. to still the mind through absent-minded doodling and allowing one to simply and fully Just Be.

BE-oodle™ – n. the mindfulness, stillness, calming feeling, and/or beauty created within one's self from simply and fully Just Being achieved through BE-oodling.

Other forms: BE-oodling

BE-oodle-ful™ – adj. (i) describing what is created by BE-oodling; (i) of having, or being filled with, the mindfulness, stillness, calming feeling, and/or beauty created within one's self from simply and fully Just Being from BE-oodling.

BE-oodling

BE-oodling

BE-oodle-ful

My List of ______________________

1 ______________________

2 ______________________

3 ______________________

4 ______________________

5 ______________________

6 ______________________

7 ______________________

8 ______________________

9 ______________________

10 ______________________

11 ______________________

MyWi
My Words, My Wisdom

Go ahead, let your wisdom out, your brilliance shine, your soul howl.
Write your own fortune cookie fortune, life mantra, quote, poem, song,
witty one-liner, sarcastic joke…you get the idea. This space - your words, your wisdom:

Quotes and poems of others are nice,
Ideas and inspiration abound.
Relying solely on them can be a vice,
For, within myself, the greatest wisdom is found.
- Kerry Raleigh

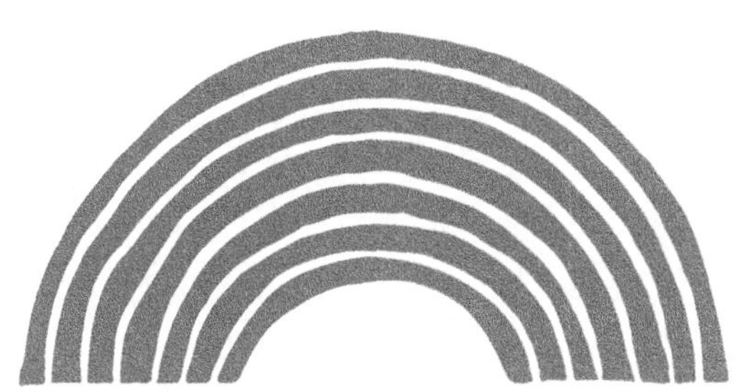

BE-oodle™

BE-oodle™ – v. to still the mind through absent-minded doodling and allowing one to simply and fully Just Be.

BE-oodle™ – n. the mindfulness, stillness, calming feeling, and/or beauty created within one's self from simply and fully Just Being achieved through BE-oodling.

Other forms: BE-oodling

BE-oodle-ful™ – adj. (i) describing what is created by BE-oodling; (i) of having, or being filled with, the mindfulness, stillness, calming feeling, and/or beauty created within one's self from simply and fully Just Being from BE-oodling.

BE-oodling

BE-oodling

BE-oodle-ful

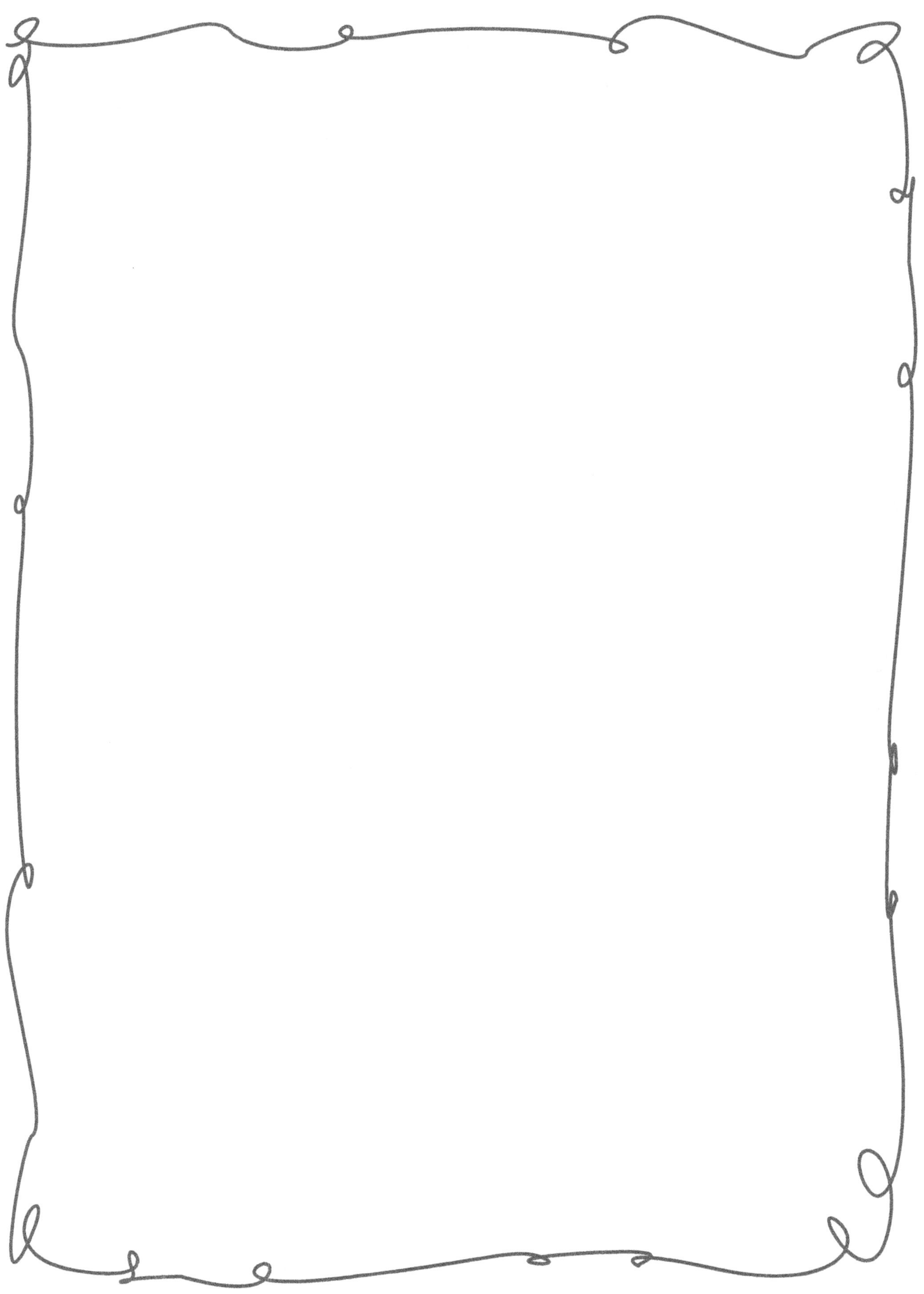

BE-oodle™

BE-oodle™ – v. to still the mind through absent-minded doodling and allowing one to simply and fully Just Be.

BE-oodle™ – n. the mindfulness, stillness, calming feeling, and/or beauty created within one's self from simply and fully Just Being achieved through BE-oodling.

Other forms: BE-oodling

BE-oodle-ful™ – adj. (i) describing what is created by BE-oodling; (i) of having, or being filled with, the mindfulness, stillness, calming feeling, and/or beauty created within one's self from simply and fully Just Being from BE-oodling.

BE-oodling

BE-oodling

BE-oodle-ful

My List of _______________

1 _______________
2 _______________
3 _______________
4 _______________
5 _______________
6 _______________
7 _______________
8 _______________
9 _______________
10 _______________
11 _______________

Go ahead, let your wisdom out, your brilliance shine, your soul howl.
Write your own fortune cookie fortune, life mantra, quote, poem, song,
witty one-liner, sarcastic joke…you get the idea. This space - your words, your wisdom:

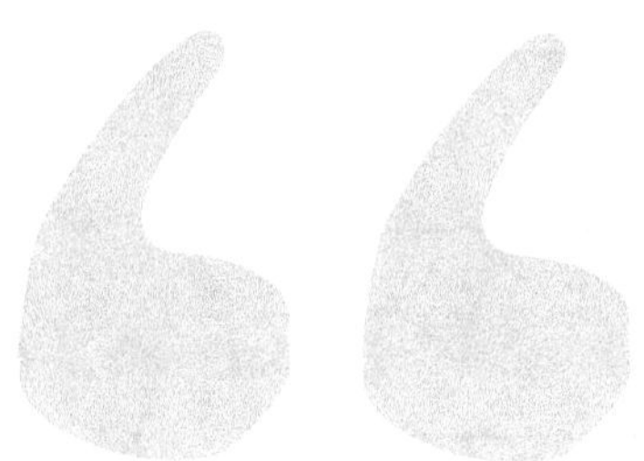

Quotes and poems of others are nice,
Ideas and inspiration abound.
Relying solely on them can be a vice,
For, within myself, the greatest wisdom is found.
- Kerry Raleigh

BE-oodle™

BE-oodle™ – v. to still the mind through absent-minded doodling and allowing one to simply and fully Just Be.

BE-oodle™ – n. the mindfulness, stillness, calming feeling, and/or beauty created within one's self from simply and fully Just Being achieved through BE-oodling.

Other forms: BE-oodling

BE-oodle-ful™ – adj. (i) describing what is created by BE-oodling; (i) of having, or being filled with, the mindfulness, stillness, calming feeling, and/or beauty created within one's self from simply and fully Just Being from BE-oodling.

BE-oodling

BE-oodling

BE-oodle-ful

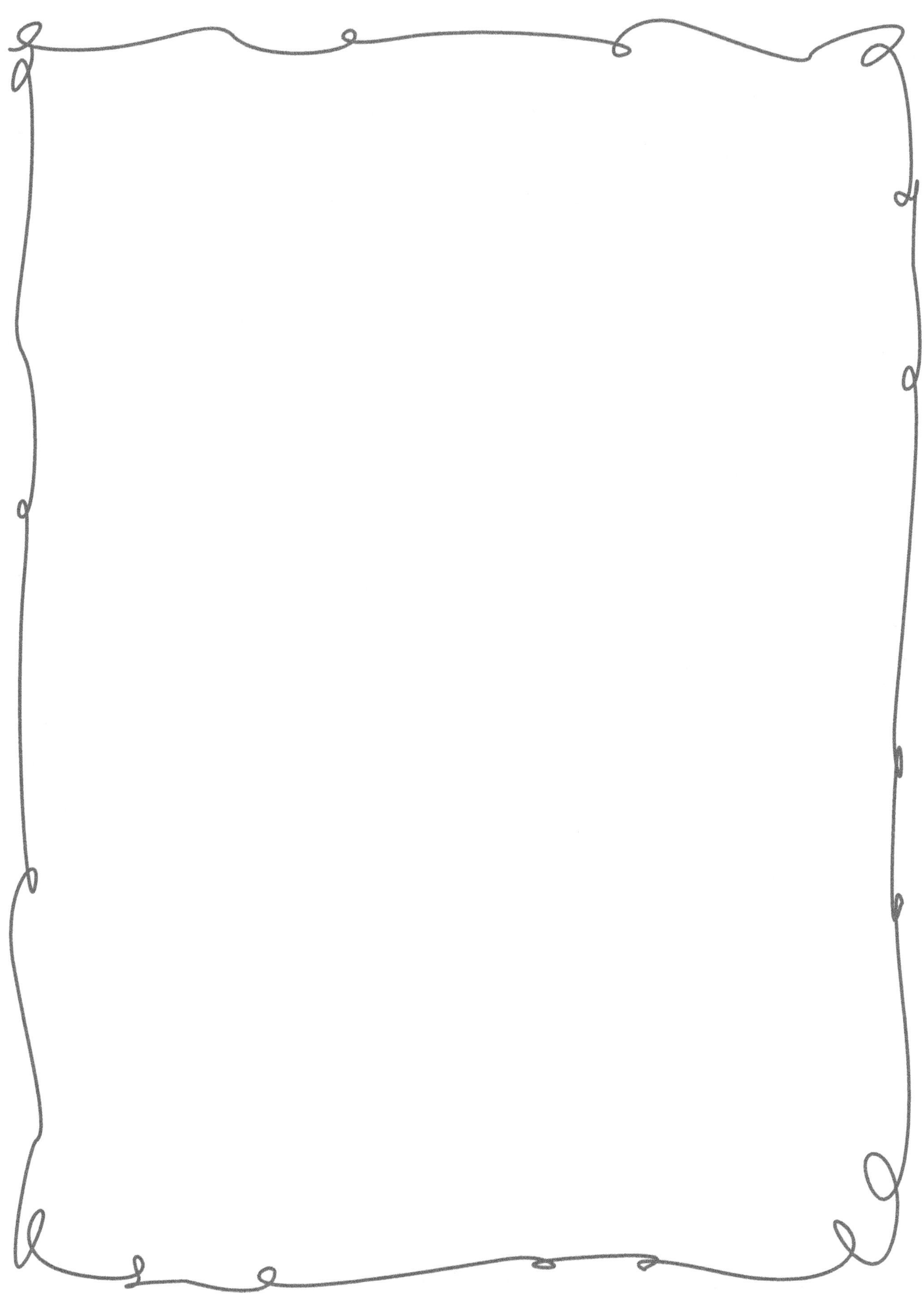

BE-oodle™

BE-oodle™ – v. to still the mind through absent-minded doodling and allowing one to simply and fully Just Be.

BE-oodle™ – n. the mindfulness, stillness, calming feeling, and/or beauty created within one's self from simply and fully Just Being achieved through BE-oodling.

Other forms: BE-oodling

BE-oodle-ful™ – adj. (i) describing what is created by BE-oodling; (i) of having, or being filled with, the mindfulness, stillness, calming feeling, and/or beauty created within one's self from simply and fully Just Being from BE-oodling.

BE-oodling

BE-oodling

BE-oodle-ful

My List of ____________________

1 ________________________

2 ________________________

3 ________________________

4 ________________________

5 ________________________

6 ________________________

7 ________________________

8 ________________________

9 ________________________

10 ________________________

11 ________________________

MyWi
My Words, My Wisdom

Go ahead, let your wisdom out, your brilliance shine, your soul howl.
Write your own fortune cookie fortune, life mantra, quote, poem, song,
witty one-liner, sarcastic joke…you get the idea. This space - your words, your wisdom:

Quotes and poems of others are nice,
Ideas and inspiration abound.
Relying solely on them can be a vice,
For, within myself, the greatest wisdom is found.
- Kerry Raleigh

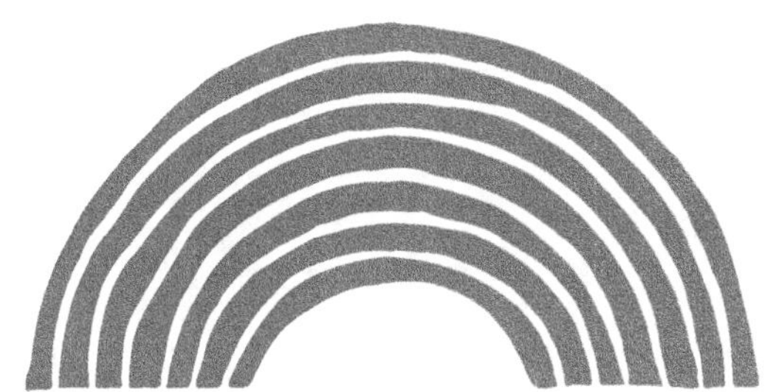

BE-oodle™

BE-oodle™ – v. to still the mind through absent-minded doodling and allowing one to simply and fully Just Be.

BE-oodle™ – n. the mindfulness, stillness, calming feeling, and/or beauty created within one's self from simply and fully Just Being achieved through BE-oodling.

Other forms: BE-oodling

BE-oodle-ful™ – adj. (i) describing what is created by BE-oodling; (i) of having, or being filled with, the mindfulness, stillness, calming feeling, and/or beauty created within one's self from simply and fully Just Being from BE-oodling.

BE-oodling

BE-oodling

BE-oodle-ful

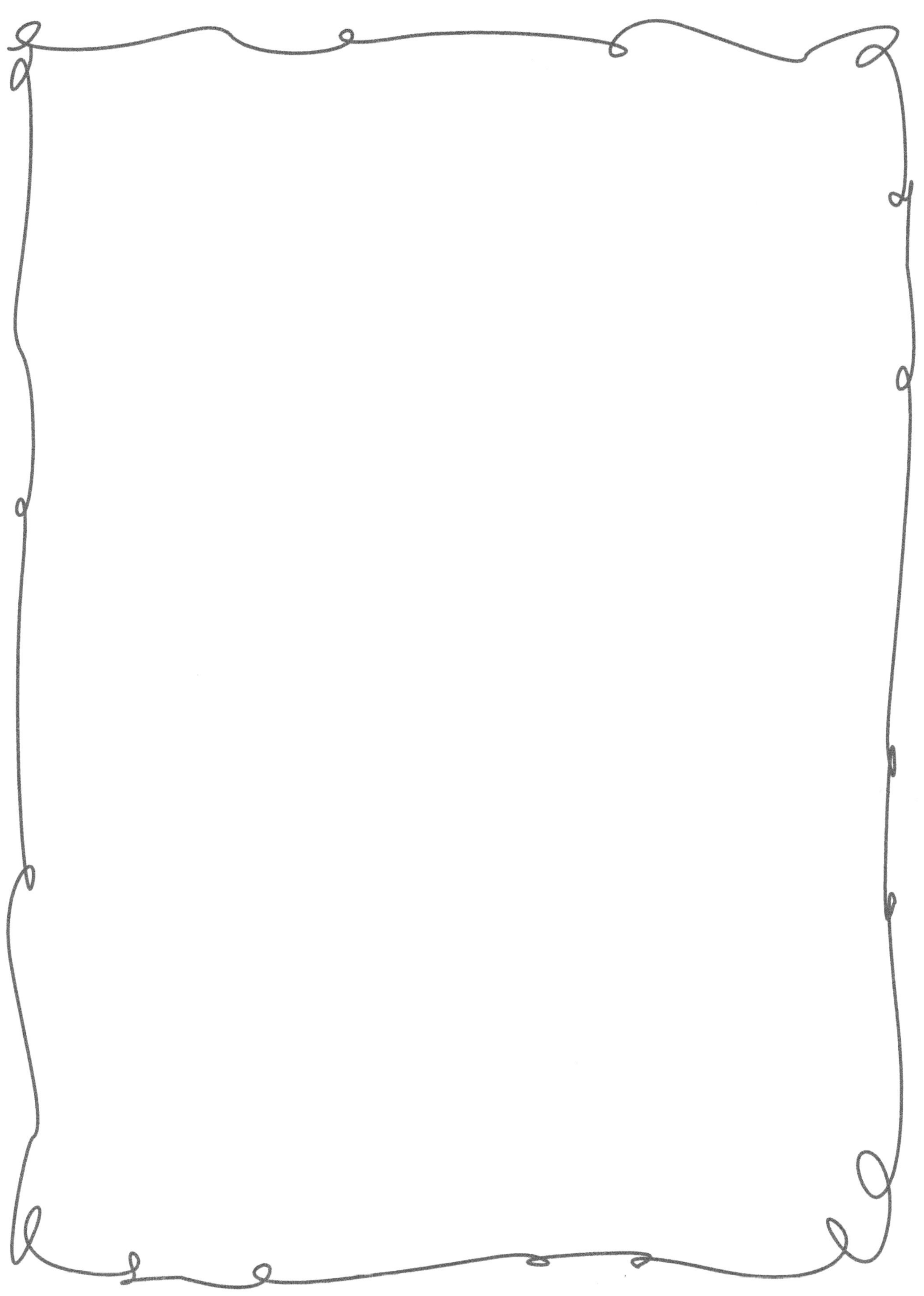

BE-oodle™

BE-oodle™ – v. to still the mind through absent-minded doodling and allowing one to simply and fully Just Be.

BE-oodle™ – n. the mindfulness, stillness, calming feeling, and/or beauty created within one's self from simply and fully Just Being achieved through BE-oodling.

Other forms: BE-oodling

BE-oodle-ful™ – adj. (i) describing what is created by BE-oodling; (i) of having, or being filled with, the mindfulness, stillness, calming feeling, and/or beauty created within one's self from simply and fully Just Being from BE-oodling.

BE-oodling

BE-oodling

BE-oodle-ful

My List of ___________________________

____

1 _______________________________________

2 _______________________________________

3 _______________________________________

4 _______________________________________

5 _______________________________________

6 _______________________________________

7 _______________________________________

8 _______________________________________

9 _______________________________________

10 _______________________________________

11 _______________________________________

MyWi
My Words, My Wisdom

Go ahead, let your wisdom out, your brilliance shine, your soul howl.
Write your own fortune cookie fortune, life mantra, quote, poem, song,
witty one-liner, sarcastic joke…you get the idea. This space - your words, your wisdom:

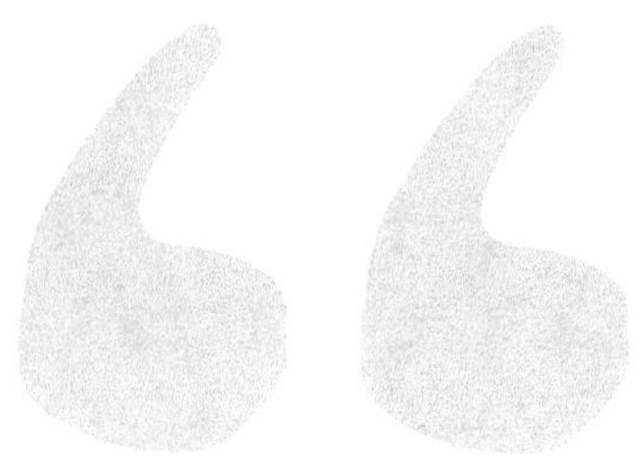

Quotes and poems of others are nice,
Ideas and inspiration abound.
Relying solely on them can be a vice,
For, within myself, the greatest wisdom is found.
- Kerry Raleigh

BE-oodle™

BE-oodle™ – v. to still the mind through absent-minded doodling and allowing one to simply and fully Just Be.

BE-oodle™ – n. the mindfulness, stillness, calming feeling, and/or beauty created within one's self from simply and fully Just Being achieved through BE-oodling.

Other forms: BE-oodling

BE-oodle-ful™ – adj. (i) describing what is created by BE-oodling; (i) of having, or being filled with, the mindfulness, stillness, calming feeling, and/or beauty created within one's self from simply and fully Just Being from BE-oodling.

BE-oodling

BE-oodling

BE-oodle-ful

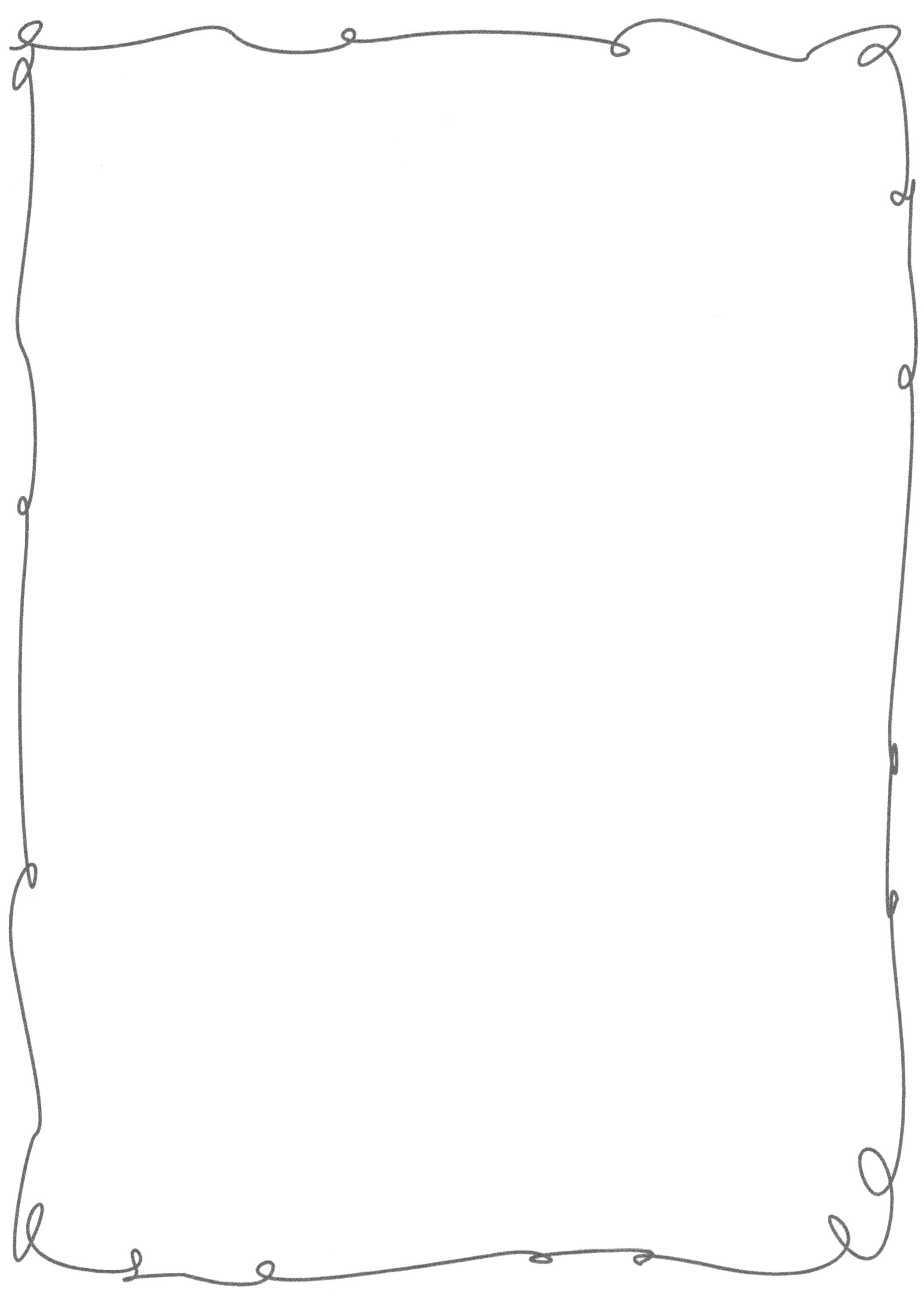

BE-oodle™

BE-oodle™ – v. to still the mind through absent-minded doodling and allowing one to simply and fully Just Be.

BE-oodle™ – n. the mindfulness, stillness, calming feeling, and/or beauty created within one's self from simply and fully Just Being achieved through BE-oodling.

Other forms: BE-oodling

BE-oodle-ful™ – adj. (i) describing what is created by BE-oodling; (i) of having, or being filled with, the mindfulness, stillness, calming feeling, and/or beauty created within one's self from simply and fully Just Being from BE-oodling.

BE-oodling

BE-oodling

BE-oodle-ful

My List of ___________________________

1 ___________________________

2 ___________________________

3 ___________________________

4 ___________________________

5 ___________________________

6 ___________________________

7 ___________________________

8 ___________________________

9 ___________________________

10 ___________________________

11 ___________________________

MyWi
My Words, My Wisdom

Go ahead, let your wisdom out, your brilliance shine, your soul howl.
Write your own fortune cookie fortune, life mantra, quote, poem, song,
witty one-liner, sarcastic joke…you get the idea. This space - your words, your wisdom:

Quotes and poems of others are nice,
Ideas and inspiration abound.
Relying solely on them can be a vice,
For, within myself, the greatest wisdom is found.
- Kerry Raleigh

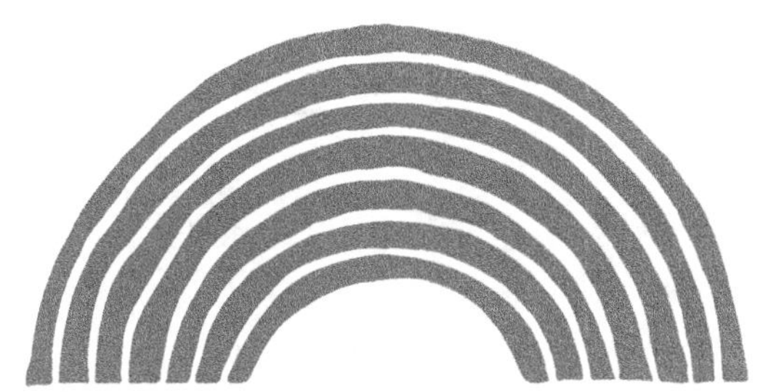

BE-oodle™

BE-oodle™ – v. to still the mind through absent-minded doodling and allowing one to simply and fully Just Be.

BE-oodle™ – n. the mindfulness, stillness, calming feeling, and/or beauty created within one's self from simply and fully Just Being achieved through BE-oodling.

Other forms: BE-oodling

BE-oodle-ful™ – adj. (i) describing what is created by BE-oodling; (i) of having, or being filled with, the mindfulness, stillness, calming feeling, and/or beauty created within one's self from simply and fully Just Being from BE-oodling.

BE-oodling

BE-oodling

BE-oodle-ful

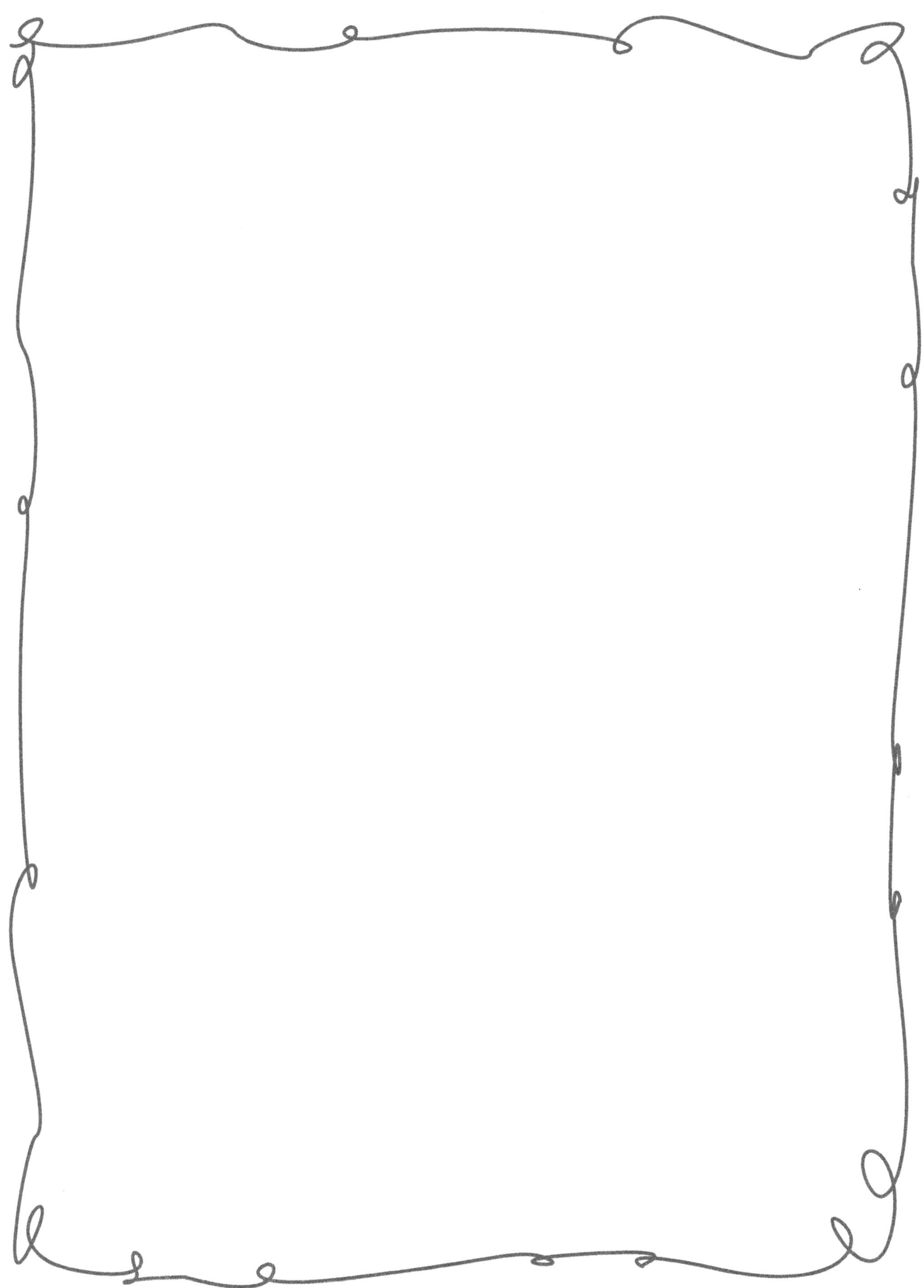

BE-oodle™

BE-oodle™ – v. to still the mind through absent-minded doodling and allowing one to simply and fully Just Be.

BE-oodle™ – n. the mindfulness, stillness, calming feeling, and/or beauty created within one's self from simply and fully Just Being achieved through BE-oodling.

Other forms: BE-oodling

BE-oodle-ful™ – adj. (i) describing what is created by BE-oodling; (i) of having, or being filled with, the mindfulness, stillness, calming feeling, and/or beauty created within one's self from simply and fully Just Being from BE-oodling.

BE-oodling

BE-oodling

BE-oodle-ful

My List of ____________________

1 ________________________

2 ________________________

3 ________________________

4 ________________________

5 ________________________

6 ________________________

7 ________________________

8 ________________________

9 ________________________

10 ________________________

11 ________________________

MyWi
My Words, My Wisdom

Go ahead, let your wisdom out, your brilliance shine, your soul howl.
Write your own fortune cookie fortune, life mantra, quote, poem, song,
witty one-liner, sarcastic joke…you get the idea. This space - your words, your wisdom:

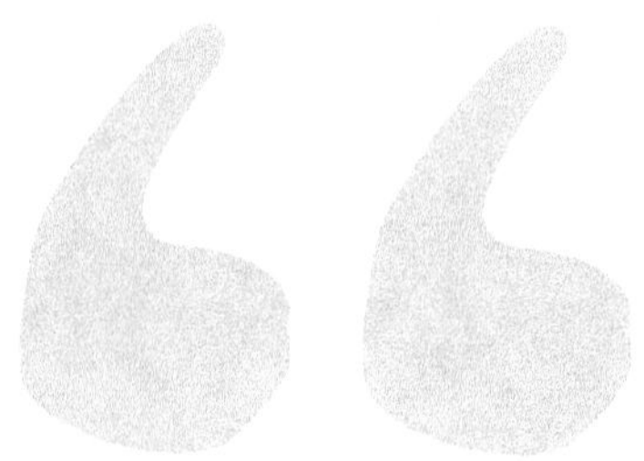

Quotes and poems of others are nice,
Ideas and inspiration abound.
Relying solely on them can be a vice,
For, within myself, the greatest wisdom is found.
- Kerry Raleigh

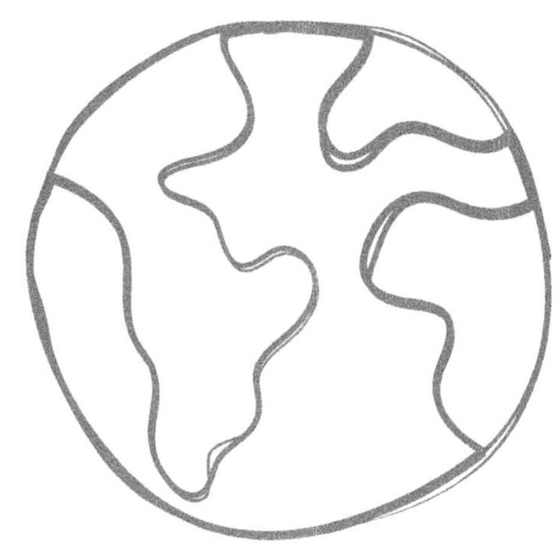

BE-oodle™

BE-oodle™ – v. to still the mind through absent-minded doodling and allowing one to simply and fully Just Be.

BE-oodle™ – n. the mindfulness, stillness, calming feeling, and/or beauty created within one's self from simply and fully Just Being achieved through BE-oodling.

Other forms: BE-oodling

BE-oodle-ful™ – adj. (i) describing what is created by BE-oodling; (i) of having, or being filled with, the mindfulness, stillness, calming feeling, and/or beauty created within one's self from simply and fully Just Being from BE-oodling.

BE-oodling

BE-oodling

BE-oodle-ful

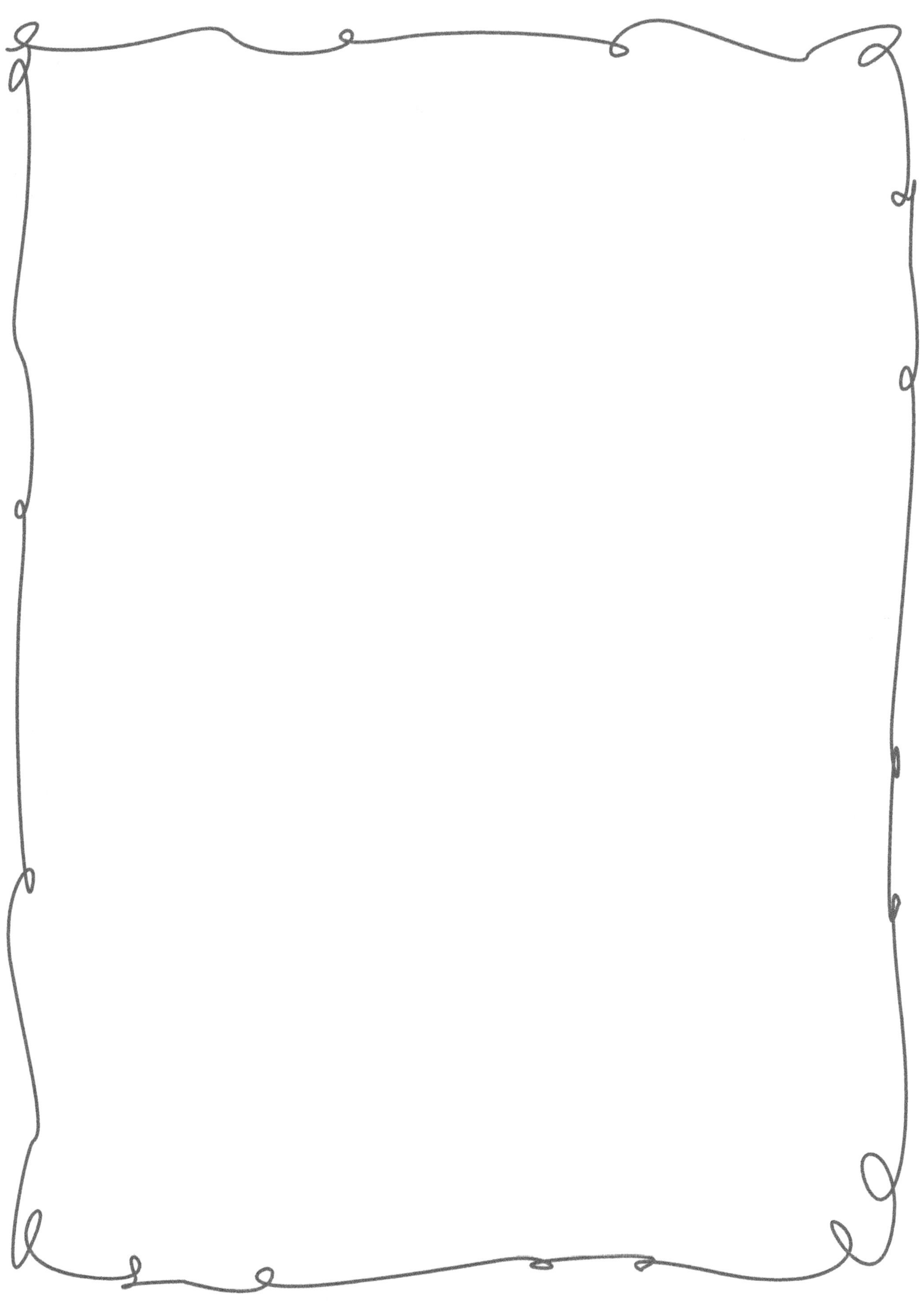

BE-oodle™

BE-oodle™ – v. to still the mind through absent-minded doodling and allowing one to simply and fully Just Be.

BE-oodle™ – n. the mindfulness, stillness, calming feeling, and/or beauty created within one's self from simply and fully Just Being achieved through BE-oodling.

Other forms: BE-oodling

BE-oodle-ful™ – adj. (i) describing what is created by BE-oodling; (i) of having, or being filled with, the mindfulness, stillness, calming feeling, and/or beauty created within one's self from simply and fully Just Being from BE-oodling.

BE-oodling

BE-oodling

BE-oodle-ful

My List of _______________

1. _______________
2. _______________
3. _______________
4. _______________
5. _______________
6. _______________
7. _______________
8. _______________
9. _______________
10. _______________
11. _______________

MyWi
My Words, My Wisdom

Go ahead, let your wisdom out, your brilliance shine, your soul howl.
Write your own fortune cookie fortune, life mantra, quote, poem, song,
witty one-liner, sarcastic joke…you get the idea. This space - your words, your wisdom:

Quotes and poems of others are nice,
Ideas and inspiration abound.
Relying solely on them can be a vice,
For, within myself, the greatest wisdom is found.
- Kerry Raleigh

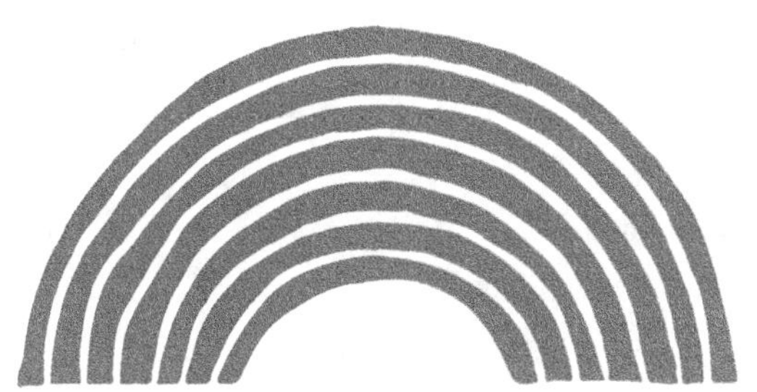

BE-oodle™

BE-oodle™ – v. to still the mind through absent-minded doodling and allowing one to simply and fully Just Be.

BE-oodle™ – n. the mindfulness, stillness, calming feeling, and/or beauty created within one's self from simply and fully Just Being achieved through BE-oodling.

Other forms: BE-oodling

BE-oodle-ful™ – adj. (i) describing what is created by BE-oodling; (i) of having, or being filled with, the mindfulness, stillness, calming feeling, and/or beauty created within one's self from simply and fully Just Being from BE-oodling.

BE-oodling

BE-oodling

BE-oodle-ful

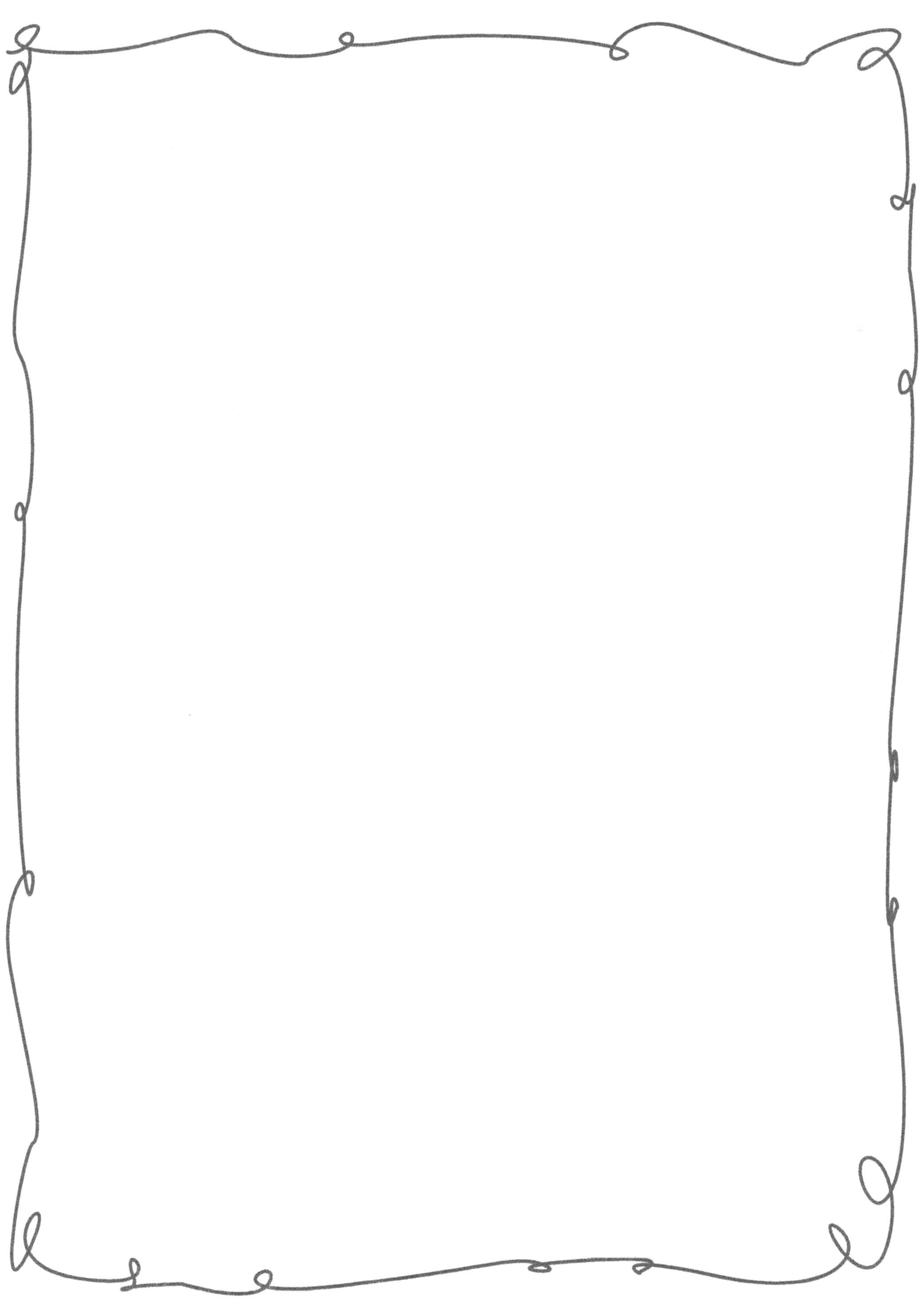

BE-oodle™

BE-oodle™ – v. to still the mind through absent-minded doodling and allowing one to simply and fully Just Be.

BE-oodle™ – n. the mindfulness, stillness, calming feeling, and/or beauty created within one's self from simply and fully Just Being achieved through BE-oodling.

Other forms: BE-oodling

BE-oodle-ful™ – adj. (i) describing what is created by BE-oodling; (i) of having, or being filled with, the mindfulness, stillness, calming feeling, and/or beauty created within one's self from simply and fully Just Being from BE-oodling.

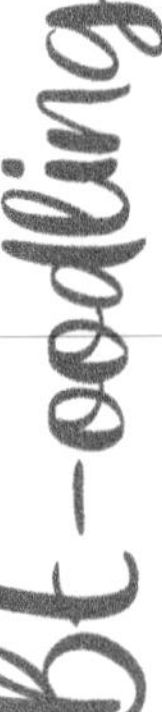

BE-oodling

BE-oodling

BE-oodle-ful

My List of ______________________________

1 ______________________________

2 ______________________________

3 ______________________________

4 ______________________________

5 ______________________________

6 ______________________________

7 ______________________________

8 ______________________________

9 ______________________________

10 ______________________________

11 ______________________________

Share

Being in 2020

Conversations
&
Connection

Love

Never underestimate the power of a good conversation

2020 is one of those years that will be talked about for generations. Will future generations refer to it as the year that changed the course of humanity? It certainly changed our individual lives and its impact continues to unfold.

For the here and now, who are you talking to about your 2020 experience? As you complete the lists in this *Being in 2020* Journal, consider having conversations.

Conversations connect.
Connection heals, restores, and strengthens:
Our belief in ourselves
Our belief in others
Our shared humanity.
With our shared humanity,
possibilities with positive outcomes emerge.

Conversations give.
A conversation holds the awareness, simple yet profound, that:
We are not alone; we are loved.
And, sometimes, that is everything.

All this from a conversation? Yes.

So, never underestimate the power of a good conversation. Likewise, never underestimate the power of self-reflection.

It's okay to use this Being in 2020 Journal as your own personal space, as conversation starters, as both, or more. If you want to have conversations with others about BEING in 2020, these pages are for you.

Connected Conversations

Use these lists to start a conversation.
And, then listen.
In listening, you are saying "You Matter".
In sharing, you are saying "I understand."

In years to come, you may want to remember
these conversations.
The following pages are for you and your
connected conversations.

Conversation Notes & Reflections

Conversation with _______________________

1. Contact this person: call, message, sit with, any way will do (well, smoke signal may be difficult and a fire hazard -- so, no smoke-signaling)
2. Select a list topic: use one from this Being in 2020 Journal or create your own
3. Give time for each person to come up with their answers
4. Write each person's list answers in the spaces below
5. Compare & Connect

List Topic: _______________________

Name _________	Me
1	
2	
3	
4	
5	
6	
7	
8	
9	
10	
11	

- - - - - - - - - Connection - - - - - - - - -

I felt connected with:

Conversation Notes & Reflections

Conversation with _______________________

    1. Contact this person: call, message, sit with, any way will do (well, smoke signal may be difficult and a fire hazard -- so, no smoke-signaling)
    2. Select a list topic: use one from this Being in 2020 Journal or create your own
    3. Give time for each person to come up with their answers
    4. Write each person's list answers in the spaces below
    5. Compare & Connect

List Topic: _______________________

Name _________	Me
1	
2	
3	
4	
5	
6	
7	
8	
9	
10	
11	

Connection

I felt connected with:

Conversation Notes & Reflections

Conversation with _______________________

1. Contact this person: call, message, sit with, any way will do (well, smoke signal may be difficult and a fire hazard -- so, no smoke-signaling)
2. Select a list topic: use one from this Being in 2020 Journal or create your own
3. Give time for each person to come up with their answers
4. Write each person's list answers in the spaces below
5. Compare & Connect

List Topic: _______________________

Name _________	Me
1	
2	
3	
4	
5	
6	
7	
8	
9	
10	
11	

- - - - - - - - - - Connection - - - - - - - - - -

I felt connected with:

Conversation Notes & Reflections

Conversation with _______________________

1. Contact this person: call, message, sit with, any way will do (well, smoke signal may be difficult and a fire hazard -- so, no smoke-signaling)
2. Select a list topic: use one from this Being in 2020 Journal or create your own
3. Give time for each person to come up with their answers
4. Write each person's list answers in the spaces below
5. Compare & Connect

List Topic: _______________________

Name _________	Me
1	
2	
3	
4	
5	
6	
7	
8	
9	
10	
11	

Connection

I felt connected with:

Conversation Notes & Reflections

Conversation with ______________________

1. Contact this person: call, message, sit with, any way will do (well, smoke signal may be difficult and a fire hazard -- so, no smoke-signaling)
2. Select a list topic: use one from this Being in 2020 Journal or create your own
3. Give time for each person to come up with their answers
4. Write each person's list answers in the spaces below
5. Compare & Connect

List Topic: ______________________

	Name __________	Me
1		
2		
3		
4		
5		
6		
7		
8		
9		
10		
11		

Connection

I felt connected with:

Conversation Notes & Reflections

Conversation with _______________

1. Contact this person: call, message, sit with, any way will do (well, smoke signal may be difficult and a fire hazard -- so, no smoke-signaling)
2. Select a list topic: use one from this Being in 2020 Journal or create your own
3. Give time for each person to come up with their answers
4. Write each person's list answers in the spaces below
5. Compare & Connect

List Topic: _______________

Name _________	Me
1	
2	
3	
4	
5	
6	
7	
8	
9	
10	
11	

- - - - - - Connection - - - - - -

I felt connected with:

Conversation Notes & Reflections

Conversation with _______________________

1. Contact this person: call, message, sit with, any way will do (well, smoke signal may be difficult and a fire hazard -- so, no smoke-signaling)
2. Select a list topic: use one from this Being in 2020 Journal or create your own
3. Give time for each person to come up with their answers
4. Write each person's list answers in the spaces below
5. Compare & Connect

List Topic: _______________________

Name _________	Me
1	
2	
3	
4	
5	
6	
7	
8	
9	
10	
11	

- - - - - - - - - - - Connection - - - - - - - - - -

I felt connected with:

Conversation Notes & Reflections

Conversation with _______________

1. Contact this person: call, message, sit with, any way will do (well, smoke signal may be difficult and a fire hazard -- so, no smoke-signaling)
2. Select a list topic: use one from this Being in 2020 Journal or create your own
3. Give time for each person to come up with their answers
4. Write each person's list answers in the spaces below
5. Compare & Connect

List Topic: _______________

Name _______	Me
1	
2	
3	
4	
5	
6	
7	
8	
9	
10	
11	

- - - - - - - Connection - - - - - - -

I felt connected with:

Conversation Notes & Reflections

Conversation with _______________________

1. Contact this person: call, message, sit with, any way will do (well, smoke signal may be difficult and a fire hazard -- so, no smoke-signaling)
2. Select a list topic: use one from this Being in 2020 Journal or create your own
3. Give time for each person to come up with their answers
4. Write each person's list answers in the spaces below
5. Compare & Connect

List Topic: _______________________

	Name _________	Me
1		
2		
3		
4		
5		
6		
7		
8		
9		
10		
11		

Connection

I felt connected with:

Conversation Notes & Reflections

Conversation with _______________________

1. Contact this person: call, message, sit with, any way will do (well, smoke signal may be difficult and a fire hazard -- so, no smoke-signaling)
2. Select a list topic: use one from this Being in 2020 Journal or create your own
3. Give time for each person to come up with their answers
4. Write each person's list answers in the spaces below
5. Compare & Connect

List Topic: _______________________

Name _________	Me
1	
2	
3	
4	
5	
6	
7	
8	
9	
10	
11	

Connection

I felt connected with:

Conversation Notes & Reflections

Conversation with _______________________

1. Contact this person: call, message, sit with, any way will do (well, smoke signal may be difficult and a fire hazard -- so, no smoke-signaling)
2. Select a list topic: use one from this Being in 2020 Journal or create your own
3. Give time for each person to come up with their answers
4. Write each person's list answers in the spaces below
5. Compare & Connect

List Topic: _______________________

Name _________	Me
1	
2	
3	
4	
5	
6	
7	
8	
9	
10	
11	

- - - - - - - - - - - Connection - - - - - - - - - - -

I felt connected with:

Conversation Notes & Reflections

Conversation with _______________________

1. Contact this person: call, message, sit with, any way will do (well, smoke signal may be difficult and a fire hazard -- so, no smoke-signaling)
2. Select a list topic: use one from this Being in 2020 Journal or create your own
3. Give time for each person to come up with their answers
4. Write each person's list answers in the spaces below
5. Compare & Connect

List Topic: _______________________

Name _________	Me
1	
2	
3	
4	
5	
6	
7	
8	
9	
10	
11	

Connection

I felt connected with:

Conversation Notes & Reflections

Conversation with _______________________

1. Contact this person: call, message, sit with, any way will do (well, smoke signal may be difficult and a fire hazard -- so, no smoke-signaling)
2. Select a list topic: use one from this Being in 2020 Journal or create your own
3. Give time for each person to come up with their answers
4. Write each person's list answers in the spaces below
5. Compare & Connect

List Topic: _______________________

Name _______	Me
1	
2	
3	
4	
5	
6	
7	
8	
9	
10	
11	

- - - - - - Connection - - - - - -

I felt connected with:

Conversation Notes & Reflections

Conversation with _______________________

1. Contact this person: call, message, sit with, any way will do (well, smoke signal may be difficult and a fire hazard -- so, no smoke-signaling)
2. Select a list topic: use one from this Being in 2020 Journal or create your own
3. Give time for each person to come up with their answers
4. Write each person's list answers in the spaces below
5. Compare & Connect

List Topic: _______________________

Name _________	Me
1	
2	
3	
4	
5	
6	
7	
8	
9	
10	
11	

- - - - - - - - - - Connection - - - - - - - - - -

I felt connected with:

Conversation Notes & Reflections

Conversation with _______________

1. Contact this person: call, message, sit with, any way will do (well, smoke signal may be difficult and a fire hazard -- so, no smoke-signaling)
2. Select a list topic: use one from this Being in 2020 Journal or create your own
3. Give time for each person to come up with their answers
4. Write each person's list answers in the spaces below
5. Compare & Connect

List Topic: _______________

Name _______	Me
1	
2	
3	
4	
5	
6	
7	
8	
9	
10	
11	

Connection

I felt connected with:

Conversation Notes & Reflections

Conversation with _______________

1. Contact this person: call, message, sit with, any way will do (well, smoke signal may be difficult and a fire hazard -- so, no smoke-signaling)
2. Select a list topic: use one from this Being in 2020 Journal or create your own
3. Give time for each person to come up with their answers
4. Write each person's list answers in the spaces below
5. Compare & Connect

List Topic: _______________

Name _________	Me
1	
2	
3	
4	
5	
6	
7	
8	
9	
10	
11	

- - - - - - - - - - Connection - - - - - - - - - -

I felt connected with:

Conversation Notes & Reflections

Conversation with _______________________

1. Contact this person: call, message, sit with, any way will do (well, smoke signal may be difficult and a fire hazard -- so, no smoke-signaling)
2. Select a list topic: use one from this Being in 2020 Journal or create your own
3. Give time for each person to come up with their answers
4. Write each person's list answers in the spaces below
5. Compare & Connect

List Topic: _______________________

Name _ _ _ _ _ _ _ _	Me
1	
2	
3	
4	
5	
6	
7	
8	
9	
10	
11	

- - - - - - - Connection - - - - - - -

I felt connected with:

Conversation Notes & Reflections

Conversation with _______________________

1. Contact this person: call, message, sit with, any way will do (well, smoke signal may be difficult and a fire hazard -- so, no smoke-signaling)
2. Select a list topic: use one from this Being in 2020 Journal or create your own
3. Give time for each person to come up with their answers
4. Write each person's list answers in the spaces below
5. Compare & Connect

List Topic: _______________________

Name _________	Me
1	
2	
3	
4	
5	
6	
7	
8	
9	
10	
11	

- - - - - - - - - - Connection - - - - - - - - - -

I felt connected with:

Conversation Notes & Reflections

Conversation with _______________

1. Contact this person: call, message, sit with, any way will do (well, smoke signal may be difficult and a fire hazard -- so, no smoke-signaling)
2. Select a list topic: use one from this Being in 2020 Journal or create your own
3. Give time for each person to come up with their answers
4. Write each person's list answers in the spaces below
5. Compare & Connect

List Topic: _______________

Name _________	Me
1	
2	
3	
4	
5	
6	
7	
8	
9	
10	
11	

- - - - - - - - - - Connection - - - - - - - - - -

I felt connected with:

Conversation Notes & Reflections

Conversation with _______________________

1. Contact this person: call, message, sit with, any way will do (well, smoke signal may be difficult and a fire hazard -- so, no smoke-signaling)
2. Select a list topic: use one from this Being in 2020 Journal or create your own
3. Give time for each person to come up with their answers
4. Write each person's list answers in the spaces below
5. Compare & Connect

List Topic: _______________________

Name __________	Me
1	
2	
3	
4	
5	
6	
7	
8	
9	
10	
11	

Connection

I felt connected with:

Conversation Notes & Reflections

Conversation with _______________________

1. Contact this person: call, message, sit with, any way will do (well, smoke signal may be difficult and a fire hazard -- so, no smoke-signaling)
2. Select a list topic: use one from this Being in 2020 Journal or create your own
3. Give time for each person to come up with their answers
4. Write each person's list answers in the spaces below
5. Compare & Connect

List Topic: _______________________

Name _________	Me
1	
2	
3	
4	
5	
6	
7	
8	
9	
10	
11	

- - - - - Connection - - - - -

I felt connected with:

Release

Reflect

Release

Reset

Be

Be

Just Be

I

Am